Natural Horsemanship

Answering the What, Why, and How for *ALL* Disciplines

By Lindsey Forkun

To my Family and Friends,

I dedicate this book to my family, friends, and my mentor Gary Convery. Gary completely overhauled my way of thinking when it comes to horses, which I am forever grateful for. My family and friends have given me continued support and this book would not have been possible without it. You have been there every step of the way to support me in my passion. I have come a long way since my parents bought me my first horse, back when I was thirteen; they would not have imagined the path it would lead me, but I can be sure that they are proud of where this path has taken me.

I give many thanks to all of those that helped with the development of this book. Many hours have been spent on photo shoots, editing, and ideas; I thank you for all of them. New students and experienced students alike, your contributions have been invaluable.

Thank you very much for your time, thoughts, encouragement, and participation.

Lindsey Forkun

www.LFEquestrian.com

AuthorHouse™
1663 Liberty Drive
Bloomington, IN 47403
www.authorhouse.com
Phone: 1-800-839-8640

First published by AuthorHouse 9/21/2009
ISBN: 978-1-4490-2093-4 (sc)
Printed in the United States of America
Bloomington, Indiana
This book is printed on acid-free paper.

Safety Note:

Please note that this book is intended as a guide only. Safety is the first priority. If you feel unsure or unsafe when working with a horse, stop, and seek a knowledgeable and experienced person to help you. Even if you feel confident in your approach, seeking professional and knowledgeable assistance can have many benefits and provide valuable insights.

NATURAL HORSEMANSHIP

Answering the What, Why, and How for ALL Disciplines

Introduction

There are so many people that profess to natural horsemanship and horse whispering that it can sometimes be difficult to understand the roots of the program and what it means to be a horse whisperer. This book will help to clarify natural horsemanship, provide an introduction on getting started, cover the basic principles surrounding natural horsemanship and provide examples and training ideas.

The natural horsemanship journey can begin at any time, for any person, and in any discipline with horses. Natural horsemanship is for people of all ages, sizes, and experience levels. Natural horsemanship is for all horses and ponies of all ages, breeds, and sizes. Natural horsemanship is for all disciplines related to our equine partners.

Throughout this book I may refer to the horse or human in the masculine context, but the material is relevant to both males and females for both humans and horses.

About Lindsey

My journey began with horses in 1992 at a small equestrian facility in the town of Uxbridge. Originally it was my older sister who took riding lessons and I was 'dragged' to the barn to watch. Every time I went to the farm with my sister my curiosity about these large animals full of power, beauty, and mystery would peak. It was March break 1992 that I decided to attend my very first horse camp and I have never looked back since.

After horse camp, I continued to ride in regular lessons at the small Uxbridge farm. In 1993 I 'officially' became hooked—I had started jumping. Some nights would be full of fun and delight aboard my favourite mounts Peanut and Digby. Other nights I'd be aboard a pokey grey pony, Chuckie, who would test my riding abilities and ultimately make me a better rider (although at the time I had been wishing I was riding peppy Peanut). I will never forget my glowing milestones: jumping a small three bar oxer (about 1.5 feet high and 3 feet wide) aboard Digby during an evening lesson. I was incredibly proud the rest of the week.

In 1993, after the small farm in Uxbridge closed, I began riding at Foxfire Equestrian Centre. Foxfire Equestrian Centre introduced me to the competitive circuit. I started with in-house schooling shows. At my very first show I rode my favourite horse, Dusty, while my sister rode a more difficult mount, April, in the same walk/trot flat class. My sister pinned 1st place while I tied for 6th of seven riders, not my most shining moment, but my very first horse show ribbon. I was delighted to have the pink ribbon with the glossy button centre bordered in a gold trim.

In later years my sister left horseback riding and took up swimming, but I became more involved with horses. I was so fortunate to have supportive parents who purchased my very first horse for me in 1998. Generals Mission was a 1994 American Quarter Horse, 15.2H bay gelding, and to me he was the cutest and most perfect horse in the world. I was at the barn every chance I could get! I could not understand how some horse owners would not be at the barn every day. I was over the moon for Mission and had many learning experiences with him. I was also very fortunate for the support given to me by my boarding stable, Foxfire Equestrian Centre. I learned about horse ownership, care and competition, and continued riding lessons from various coaches at the farm.

I began competing more often and at more prestigious shows once I had Mission. With Mission I started to realize I had a natural ability to train horses. On my own I trained Mission in competitive trail and western speed events. With the help of lessons I trained Mission to jump. I started showing with the Durham Saddle Club series where we were awarded numerous titles including the Charlie's Pride Memorial Award for Versatility two years in a row as well as titles in hunter over fences, showmanship, English Flat, Western Flat, Speed Events and Competitive Trail. I also competed with the Uxbridge Horseman's Association and achieved a year-end award for overall youth performance. My abilities had improved so much, that during competition it was more a question of what ribbon would I get, rather then the question I had been asking 'would I place at all?'

Then in 1999 a seemingly terrible thing happened. Foxfire Equestrian Centre sold and I had to move Mission to a new farm. I was devastated. I loved the people, the horses, and the facility and was very sad to leave. However, leaving Foxfire opened the door to new exciting and challenging opportunities as well as finding a new path to working with horses.

In 1999 I moved to a couple of farms trying to find the right balance of cost, distance, and facilities. It was a small farm in Greenbank that seemed to have all the right pieces and was where I picked up dressage. My first dressage lessons were the very first time that I began to understand having contact with the horse's mouth and collecting the horse with leg and body rather than solely with the hand. I enrolled in Pony Club, which allowed me to go to many clinics with various coaches. I achieved levels D, D1, and D2 in the one year that I was with Pony Club. I also competed in starter level show jumping for the very first time, and was champion at almost every qualifier, champion at the central championships, and 1st overall for central Ontario. I was invited to the Central Canadian Show Jumping Championships to compete for the Central Ontario team, where my team finished second. Mission and I traveled all over Ontario competing in our various events and participating in the diverse clinics.

In late 2000, I moved to a farm just outside of Claremont. This was the year that I took part in the movie *Prancer Returns*, riding Mission in the parade scene. After the farm changed hands I moved to another farm in northern Uxbridge and I competed in the 2002 Canadian National Exhibition in Toronto (CNE). I was 11th in children's hunter with my new horse, Mission Accomplished, who had never shown at a recognized show before, and who had only been jumping for a couple months. I also competed with the Durham Saddle Club and brought home 11 trophies and 3 ribbons from several different classes and divisions, including the Charlie's Pride Memorial Award for Versatility. I also made the very difficult decision to sell Mission in 2002 in order to advance my riding with my Hanoverian cross mare Mission Accomplished. Mission sold to a loving family who became my clients for horse training and lessons, as they were so pleased with the training I had done with Mission.

In 2002 I reached a critical turning point in the way I worked with horses. It all started with a large metal box atop four wheels. At the time I was convinced this contraption was the work of the devil, but now I know it was just a trailer. I struggled with loading my horses on trailers, and horses that'd previously given no protest were getting worse.

I tried everything: lunge whips, lunge lines around the rump pushing the horse in, buckets of treats, and more. I remember having trailer practice sessions that would take hours and the horse would be no better with loading afterwards. Once I had figured out a way to force a horse to get on, they would stop even further from the trailer and there was no budging them. This is when I had to reflect and thought that there must be a better way. I was desperate to find answers, and as the saying goes 'where there is a will there is a way.'

I found an incredible answer that was really quite unknown and secretive at the time: natural horsemanship. Natural horsemanship held the answers to all of my questions and problems and forever changed me. All of a sudden I could remember times when my horse had been trying to communicate with me, but I had been oblivious that there were communication signals even taking place! This was the start of a lifelong journey; a journey of change, of reflection, learning, and patience.

It was through my connections at the farm in Claremont that I moved down the road to Pleasure Valley and had my first introduction to local horse whispering legend Gary Convery. I was extremely fortunate to have the opportunity to work side by side with Gary for three years helping with trail rides, horse handling, horse training, barn help, children's summer camps, and anything else he needed. Gary completely overhauled my way of working with horses. He taught me to read a horse in a way I had never done before.

I had already been curious about natural horsemanship and had read about it, but this was my first chance at personal feedback, asking questions, and witnessing natural horsemanship first hand. I discovered the use of a rope halter and advanced my learning. This was the year I founded my own company, Lindsey Forkun Equestrian, on the motto 'helping you do better.'

Over the summer of 2003, my students and I went to many shows, doing extremely well. I competed in child/adult jumpers and was 4th overall on the Trillium circuit with Amber, and was invited to the championships to represent central Ontario. I also was invited to the Tournament of Champions in 2003. Over the season I had many more accomplishments including winning the 3'6" open jumper derby.

In 2004, each of my students who tried for Trillium year-end awards wound up finishing in the top ten. It was an excellent season with many champion and reserve champion Trillium ribbons. I showed the horse 'Boys Knight Out' at Trillium at Palgrave Phase II in August at his first Trillium show. He won the stake class and wound up reserve champion in the division. My students with Mission also picked up some champion and reserve champion titles on the Trillium hunter circuit. This was a very successful season and yet also a very sad one because it was my last show season before university.

I sold both my horses and enrolled at the University of Ontario Institute of Technology for the B.Sc.N. four-year degree. Despite not owning any horses, I continued to coach and train for clients and also started services related to selling horses for people. This was my way of being able to ride horses while in university because I would test ride the horses, show the horses to clients, and do some training. I have continued this service because of all the networking I've established, my match making abilities, and my successful website.

My team of students showed at Durham Saddle Club in 2005 where they were all in the top two for at least one of their classes. I also showed a green horse for his first full season, Top Secret Mission, who was reserve champion overall in the senior division. It was difficult commuting between university and home for riding, but I found a way to make it work.

However, an unanticipated sorrow that same year struck a serious blow when Gary Convery passed away over the Christmas holidays. My mentor, my teacher, my role model and my leader... just gone. It was a loss that hit me hard, and his family much harder. He was loved and respected by many. I am thankful for the time I did have with Gary and regret not having had more opportunity to study with him. Gary's passing pushed me to look for further mentorship, which steered me to Parelli Natural Horsemanship.

During 2006 a variety of my students competed on different circuits, placing well with many champion and reserve champion titles. I continued to work with Parelli Natural Horsemanship and incorporated this training with the other natural horseman techniques I have studied. I also became certified as a coach through the Canadian Coaches Association in the sport of Equestrian.

In 2007 I was hired back at Pleasure Valley as coach and horse trainer. I developed my skills with gaited breeds including Paso Fino, Kentucky Mountain, and Tennessee Walker horses. I was in my final year of university and working with my two new horses, Ely and Canterbury. I obtained my Parelli Level 1 with Ely and worked on Level 2 with both horses. I also did some showing, receiving the champion award at Canterbury's first show.

The next year was incredibly busy, but not just with horses. I graduated from university, got married, obtained my Ontario Equestrian Federation Level 8 (currently the highest English riding level you can test for), sold Ely to a student, worked with a new horse I had purchased in 2007,

Elegance, began coaching for York Equestrian Riding School, and continued working for Pleasure Valley. The show season was interrupted because of my life milestones but many shows were still attended and accomplishments included placing at the CNE in the hack division with Elegance when it was only her third show!

Heading into 2009 I have one final step to complete my Ontario Equestrian Federation Coaching Level 1, which I hope to have completed by 2010. I own and work with Elegant Lady Cheltenham and Killarney to Here. I coach for York Equestrian Riding School, coach and train for Pleasure Valley, as well as doing freelance work training many 'problem' horses, 'hot' horses, gaited horses, pleasure horses, and hunter/jumper competition horses, and coaching for riders and handlers. Horses remain my job of passion while I maintain a full time position as a Public Health Nurse for the Regional Municipality of Durham.

Lindsey's other horse experience includes:

- Operating Lindsey Forkun Equestrian since 2002
- Obtaining her Ontario Equestrian Federation Rider Level 8 in 2008
- Obtaining her Parelli Natural Horsemanship Level 1 in 2007
- Judging and coaching at New Era Farms from 1999-2007
- Finalist for the Canadian National Top 20 Under 20 Leadership and Innovation Award for her work with horses in 2005
- Volunteering as the English Director, head of the Youth Committee and Newsletter Editor for the Durham Saddle Club in 2000 and 2001
- Volunteering over 200 hours at YMCA riding camps in 1999
- Volunteering at T.R.A.C.K (a therapeutic riding association for challenged kids) in 1999

Pictures of Lindsey

1. Lindsey with a team of students (including Mission on the far right)
2. Lindsey riding Mission in the movie Prancer Returns for the parade scene
3. Lindsey riding Thetis with no bridle/hackamore
4. Lindsey competing in show jumping with Amber
5. Lindsey with a team of students at the horse palace in Toronto, Ontario
6. Lindsey swimming with Canterbury
7. Lindsey and Canterbury are champions in hunter

4.

1.

2.

5.

3.

6.

7.

THE WHAT

Love it or hate it, you have to admit that natural horsemanship is gaining popularity all over the world—and furthermore, the professionals who use it are very impressive with their horses!

What is Natural Horsemanship and the Fine Art of Horse Whispering?

Natural horsemanship simply means communicating with horses. This is done by listening to the horse's body language and responding in a way that mimics how horses communicate with each other in their natural environment. Natural horsemanship is using communication to work with horses rather than intimidation and fear. Being a horse whisperer means knowing how to communicate effectively with your horse and how to become a leader for your horse.

Natural horsemanship is an art learned through dedication, patience and education. Learning to read a horse's communication signals, understanding how to communicate with horses, learning the basic principles and developing a partnership require skill, perseverance, and most especially, an open mind.

When you work with a horse naturally, it means you are communicating through body language using basic cues that allow you to have a conversation with your horse. This has many added benefits. Unlike some horse handlers, you won't need a clicker or a bag of treats to get your horse's cooperation. You'll also be able to ask your horse for more complex tasks or to work with you in more difficult scenarios. Once the foundation is laid, you will progress more quickly with your horse and be able to advance in completing tasks that the intimidator style of handler can only dream of.

The leadership role of the handler is one that preserves the horse's dignity by allowing the horse to make decisions, mistakes, corrections, and most importantly, to have responsibilities. Allowing your horse to be a partner in the relationship means you respect what your horse has to offer in the partnership and you value your horse's input.

Letting the horse take the lead sometimes:

•The horse may start to test the handler and take longer to respond to requests because the horse doesn't recognize your leadership.

Letting the horse take the lead more often:

•The horse may test your leadership often and will start to question any requests you make. The horse may get upset if you try to change the routine.

Letting the horse take the lead most of the time:

• The horse may become quite nervous and skittish from not having a capable leader.

Natural horsemanship is fair, focused, and universal. It works with all equine partners. When you practice natural horsemanship you have to go against human predator instincts to trap, control, and force a horse into behaving the way we want. Instead, the focus is on partnership; you are the leader that **causes** and **permits** the horse to perform and react in a desired way.

A traditional intimidator style leader would focus on **forcing** a horse do something, but equally harmful are people who let their horses take the lead because they're afraid of offending or hurting the horse. **Letting** a horse do whatever he wants will instill superiority and eventually fear in the horse and can potentially be dangerous for the person. Horses need and want to be safe and to feel secure.

One objective of natural horsemanship is to move away from letting or forcing our horses to do things, and instead put the focus on causing and permitting. Luckily for us, horses are prey animals that naturally look for a leader to keep them safe. If you can be that leader, then horses will willingly follow you and take your direction.

All horses have different temperaments which will determine how confident, focused, and competent a leader they require. Some horses may continually test your competence in order to

Forcing the horse to do things sometimes:

•The horse can become distrusting of the handler and may test the handler more often.

Forcing the horse to do things more often:

•The horse can become irritable and distrusting of humans. The horse may show signs of agitation such as swishing his tail or pinning his ears.

Forcing the horse to do things most of the time:

•The horse can get quite agitated and even aggressive in attempts to avoid the handler. The horse will lose his will to please, and this will affect what you can do with your horse.

ensure their safety/rank in the herd. Herds naturally have a pecking order. Take a moment to observe horses in their paddocks with their herd mates and you'll discover the personalities and the rank of the horses within the herd.

Working with horses naturally will allow you to problem solve on your own because you'll have a foundation of knowledge to draw from. This means when something goes wrong, you will understand what your horse is saying, what the root cause is, and how to address it as a fair leader. Natural horsemanship puts a focus on understanding horse psychology so you can anticipate, recognize, and solve problems before they happen. A major focus of natural horsemanship is safety. Working with a horse naturally helps make an environment with horses much safer because the horse is more likely to stay in a thinking frame of mind rather than reverting to a more primitive frame of mind, fight-or-flight.

As well, the handler learns to read horse behavior and recognizes tension before it becomes a problem and can address it in a safe and effective way. When working with horses, it's important to remember that the horse is independent, with his own thoughts, feelings, fears, desires, and goals. That's why putting an emphasis on understanding horses, communicating with the horse, and being a leader for the horse are so important and essential when working with horses in any discipline in order to achieve the best results.

The Basic Principles of Natural Horsemanship

1. The goal is communication, not intimidation. When working with horses you should always be thinking about what your body language and cues are saying to the horse and what the horse is saying to you.

2. The leader's space takes priority. This translates into meaning that the leader can move whomever he wants in the herd; the leader can touch whomever he wants in the herd; the leader will protect the space of his followers and himself; and the leader will not move out of the way for anyone, any horse, or any other animal.

3. Start with your ideal cue. Always start with your ideal cue and then ask fairly, ask gently, ask firmly, and reward greatly when you get the correct answer. Follow this progression when asking your horse something so that he understands that you are consistent and fair in your approach. As a result your horse will start to be more aware of your ideal cues and react to them appropriately. This also follows the premises that it is comfortable to do the right thing and uncomfortable to do the wrong thing. By starting with your ideal cue and then increasing the intensity of the cue, you help your horse realize what you want by making the correct response comfortable and the wrong response progressively more uncomfortable.

4. The reward is in the release. Remember that when you stop asking something of your horse, it must be because the horse was correct, not because you gave up. This is so important and often the one principle that many people have problems with. Have

confidence in yourself that you are asking correctly. Be patient enough to wait for the correct response.

5. Encounter, Wait, Revisit. Putting this into practice means that if a horse stops/avoids something scary, ALLOW the horse to stay at a distance comfortable to him, keep him still and facing the scary area. Then when the horse is ready (he will show some sign of being calmer or will ask you a question) you can back up or do a small circle and then revisit the scary area/object. When the horse is ready he will cross the boundary and proceed safely past whatever is scary. If you just kick him forward he may turn to his fight-or-flight instincts and go running and/or bucking past whatever he thinks is scary. This applies to anything scary or something that the horse feels he lacks the confidence to do. For example, he may stop at a jump because he thinks it is too high to jump, or because it is a scary shape. Respond to this type of situation in the same way: wait and then revisit.

6. Geared toward a goal. Your horse should always be able to find comfort or release of pressure because there should always be a purpose or goal that you're working towards. That's why smacking a horse repeatedly for doing something wrong is very unnatural and unjust. If there isn't a movement or task the horse can do to get the handler to stop the action, then there isn't a goal in mind and the handler is being unfair. This principle also refers to the handler always having a focus in mind. This means that the handler is the leader and has a plan for the moment and the future. The plan could be 'we will stand here and eat grass' or more complex like 'let's perform a canter figure eight pattern with three flying lead changes through the middle'. The point is that the handler is to be the leader, so they must always have in mind what the focus in on. Horses often test leaders by trying to change their focus such as turning in to the middle of an arena when not asked, cutting corners in the arena, breaking out of gait, etc. Your horse should always be able to understand the current focus or goal at hand.

7. Act like your horse's partner. Most importantly in natural horsemanship is the recognition that the horse is primarily a prey animal, and the human is primarily a predator. It's important to turn this prey and predator relationship into a partner relationship. Try to understand your horse and learn to recognize the difference between a horse asking for clarification versus a horse misbehaving, being scared, or confused. Learning common communication signals will help you develop this skill.

Basic Horse Psychology

We've established that everything about horses comes down to one simple fact: the horse is a prey animal. Horses are most concerned about being eaten by something else. That's why they want a competent leader, to keep them safe. Stallions are a little bit different. They may be prey animals, but they're also biologically programmed to be leaders to protect the herd. Proving your leadership to a stallion will likely be more difficult than recruiting a mare or gelding.

If a horse feels safe with a leader, he'll **want** to follow the leader; that's basic horse psychology. There's a huge difference between wanting to work for a handler and being forced to follow a handler. When a horse wants to work for you, he'll learn intently without much resistance. When the horse is reluctantly following you, he'll do as little as possible to get the job done so he can get back to his paddock or stall. This can mean the difference between a clear round with a fast time in a jump off, or just a clear round with a mediocre time because the horse is too busy swishing his tail at you in protest. If your horse is your willing partner, he'll offer perfect lead changes, more height during piaffe, a faster spin or better ground manners, all because he wants to please you!

Horses have two different mindsets. A horse can either be in:

1) a thinking frame of mind, or

2) in a fight-or-flight frame of mind.

Thinking Frame of Mind:
- Low headset
- Relaxed ears
- Relaxed tail
- It is fairly easy to get the horse's attention
- Making no loud noises, but may make soft noises
- Focused
- Relaxed steps and movements

Temporary Distraction:
- Higher headset
- Ears fixed on something
- Relaxed / slightly raised tail
- Making little or no noise
- The horse can listen to you
- The horse is focused on something else
- May take some quick or tense steps
- You can get the horse's attention with some effort

Fight-or-Flight Mindset:
- High headset
- Animated ears
- Tail is tucked or animated
- The horse might call, neigh, blow, or snort
- It is difficult to get the horse to respond to cues
- The horse's attenion wanders
- The horse is not focused
- The horse makes quick and/or animated movements

When a horse is in a thinking frame of mind, the horse is calm, relaxed, and able to follow cues, learn, and listen. When a horse gets nervous, anxious, and/or scared, the horse can turn to the fight -or-flight frame of mind where he is on high alert and feels his safety is threatened. A horse in fight-or-flight mode will primarily be looking for a way to run from what is scary and secondarily for a way to fight what is scary. Generally a horse's first response when scared is to run. Only if the horse is trapped, confined, or can't see a way out will he fight by biting, kicking or striking out when scared. However, horses may use biting, kicking or striking out when in a thinking mode in order to protect their personal space. Learning the communication signals of horses will make it easy for you to tell the difference between a scared horse, and one in a thinking frame of mind.

When observing a herd of horses, you can tell which horse is dominant based on who moves who, but also from who protects their personal space. Protecting your personal space means more than what humans consider personal space. The average human in North America will determine their personal space as an arm length. Horses however, on average, determine their personal space to be about a ten-foot circle of space around them. This means you need to be aware of the ten feet around you and be able to maintain control over that space.

Horses determine a leader based on both the protection of personal space and the ability to move another horse/human. When a herd boss moves another horse, it could be by pinning his ears, threatening to bite, or actually kicking or biting another horse. The dominant horse may move a horse because he wants to play, take their food, or just confirm his rank in the herd.

A submissive horse that comes up to you in the field should stop about ten feet away and allow you to approach him, or the horse should only approach you if you are signaling it is okay to do so. You can signal to a horse it is okay to enter your space by relaxing your stance and turning a foot out to the side, leaning back slightly, and/or by doing your cue for 'come'.

Reading horse behaviour starts with observing horses and studying their body language. You want to look at the body as a sum of individual parts. Look at the manner a horse approaches another:

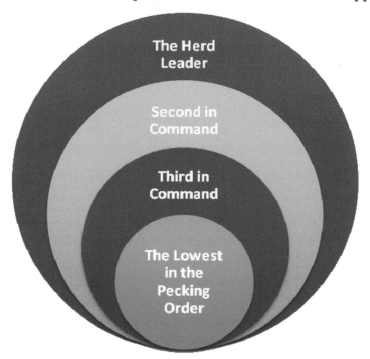

the tension in the body; how high or low the head is; if the tail is swishing; the movement of the ears and the lips. Combine all of these signals to learn how horses communicate. Also learn the progression of signals. What is the first signal a horse gives before carrying through with an action? For example, when a horse goes to move another horse away from a pile of hay, note the pinned ears, the quickened footsteps, and tensed body that are all warning signs before the horse actually tries to bite. In many cases, a horse will have a tense body for several minutes before actually kicking or biting—can you spot this?

Natural horsemanship mimics this progression of cues. For example, when asking a horse to go forward when riding, you would first ask with a light squeeze from your legs, then a firm squeeze, then a little kick, then a swing of a crop/rope, and finally to a tap behind the rider's leg with the crop/rope. The progression is fair, sequential and consistent. Just like the horse will give the same warning signals every time before they kick or bite, the natural horseman will do this too.

Every herd has a definite rank. The dominant horse can move all other horses. The second-in-command can move all horses except the leader and so forth until you get to the horse lowest in the pecking order. Sometimes horses may share a rank with another horse and may continually fluctuate in their standing within the herd. This generally happens with horses lower in the pecking order that are struggling not to be the bottom horse.

Geldings can be more dominant in a herd if they have a mare they become attached to, or if they were gelded late and retain stallion-like traits. Generally mixing mares and geldings is not a problem, but some facilities choose to keep mares and geldings separate to prevent horse couples getting too attached or geldings from becoming too protective of their mares.

To learn more about herd dominance and herd dynamics, take a moment to observe horses in the paddock. Introduce a new horse to a paddock of horses to more easily observe the ritual of determining rank (be sure the paddock is large enough for all of the horses, and be sure not to out match the new horse i.e. introducing an old horse into a group of 6-7 young horses may not be a good idea without some intermediary steps first). The dominant horse will usually do one of two things:

1) protect his herd by keeping himself in between his herd and the new horse, or

2) he will refuse to move in any great depth and will wait for the new horse to come closer because no horse should be able to move the dominant horse.

Note that usually the horse low in the pecking order is the first to meet the new horse in a paddock. This is because they are anxious to determine if:

1) this leader can be better than his current leader, or

2) he is trying to determine if this is his chance to dominate over another horse within the herd.

The new horse to the herd will usually take a day or two to establish the current pecking order and the characters of the horses in the field. After a couple of days the new horse will make a move for a more dominant position in the herd if he desires.

You will also note that there is strength in numbers. A large herd of more than eight horses will usually be more wary of newcomers to the group, and new members of the group will take longer to rise to the top of the order. Also, the longer the group has been together, the closer friends they will generally be.

I have observed this at many places and the most interesting to me are the herds at Pleasure Valley. They have very large paddocks of several acres. There is a herd of geldings that grew up together as yearlings and two year olds. Several years later, the horses are very close and new members of the herd are accepted but usually kept at the periphery. It's also interesting that a member of the herd can leave for a few months and return to the same rank as when he left. This is also true for the mares' paddock, which clearly has a close group, comprised of some horses that grew up together and another periphery group of horses that were added later.

It's unknown if horses feel love the way humans do, and if they feel love towards humans. What is certain is that horses can have respect, trust, and fondness towards humans and other horses. Fondness towards humans is demonstrated by numerous horse whisperers around the world including famous names like Monty Roberts, Pat Parelli, Linda Parelli, John Lyons, and many more. Watching the relationships with their horses at liberty, you can see firsthand the trust and respect as the horses try willingly and with all their effort to learn, perform, and follow their fair and great leaders. Observe fondness as a horse chooses to come to his owner at liberty—without the use of treats or trickery, or watch as a horse nickers to his handler as a friendly hello, and acknowledges his handler with preference over another person. Fondness towards certain horses is shown through preference of a grazing buddy or grooming partner, or the soft nicker to a friend passing by or the loud calling to a horse friend that has gone out of sight.

I remember back when Foxfire Equestrian Centre had sold, I decided to move my horse, Mission, to the same farm where a close friend had moved her horse, Phantom. My friend moved a month earlier than I, but the day Mission and I showed up at the new farm, Phantom was turned out in his paddock and came running over to the gate to greet Mission. It was so nice to see that they remembered each other. Phantom and Mission showed so often together and were used to many horses coming and going on horse trailers, that typically a horse arriving at the farm would be uneventful and not worthy of running to the gate for. Paired with his nicker for Mission, I knew these buddies remembered each other and were happy to see each other.

All horses have different personalities, or I guess you could say 'horsealities', just like humans. There are shy horses, brave horses, curious horses, skittish horses, submissive horses, and dominant horses.

A shy horse is one that lacks confidence and is looking for a strong leader. Once a shy horse has found a leader, he is very willing to please, but may test the leader often just to put his mind at ease that he's made the right leader choice. Shy horses can be recognized because they find it difficult to look a human straight on with both eyes (the horse's body will face the human, but the horse will turn their head to one side, as if looking behind them or off to one side). They will also give in to flight easily, and may be reluctant to allow you to touch them in their delicate areas (around the eyes, ears, and tail). Weak leadership with a shy horse will make the horse worried and he will have a tendency to go into fight-or-flight mode more often.

Confident horses willingly enter new situations and the leader must be careful to protect the horse from danger, or his confidence can be shattered as well as his confidence in the leader. For example, a horse may confidently approach you in the paddock, but if the horse gets bitten or kicked by another horse when you, as the leader, did nothing to protect him, then the confidence will be damaged in your relationship with that horse. After all, if you cannot even protect the horse from his herd mates, how are you going to protect the horse from a wolf or bear? Another example would be if you asked your horse to jump a difficult fence and the horse does so willingly but ends up tangled up in the fence. This could make the horse both scared of you as the leader and also of jumping.

Submissive horses will rarely contest your attempts to be leader, while more dominant horses may test you more often because they're looking for their chance to be leader. You have to prove to the dominant horse that you can stand your ground and that you are a knowledgeable leader. Once you have done this you may be tested occasionally to be sure you're doing a better job than he could be doing. Weak leadership towards a dominant horse will cause the horse to become more assertive and he will start to take over in choosing what to do and how fast to do it.

There are sensitive horses that will react to the slightest cues and they are always looking for communication. Then there are less responsive horses that may require a more dramatic cue, or more motivation in order to respond to cues.

When working with or purchasing a horse, it is important to have a horse with a character that suits your own. If you are a person who talks with your hands and makes big body movements, then a sensitive horse is probably not the best choice. If you are very aware of your body movements and enjoy using subtle cues, then a sensitive horse might work perfectly for you.

Choosing a Horse to Suit You

There are three main criteria for judging the suitability of a horse for you: confidence, dominance, and sensitivity.

Confidence

Confidence can sometimes be described as bravery. It's largely a product of environment, but horses are all born with different amounts of confidence. Some horses can build confidence more easily than others, and some are more easily intimidated. All breeds of horses can be either extremely confident or extremely skittish. Because environment and upbringing are directly related to a horse's confidence, it's important to socialize a horse from a young age. Introduce horses to as many things as possible such as tarps, umbrellas, bridges, water, hoses, clippers, trailers, poles, flowers, trails, radios, cars, and other things that are noisy, moving, or different from everyday experiences.

One easy thing you can do to help build confidence is to change things in the paddock or working area bi-weekly: add a new toy; add coloured poster board to the arena/fence wall; rearrange jumps/flowers; put a barrel in a field; or do something different so that the horse can become comfortable with change on a regular basis. Horses easily fall into routine and if a horse is used to being worked in an area that is set up a certain way, it can be quite nerve-racking for him when it's changed. For example, if in an arena the jumps are always placed and/or stored the same way, then the horse may become anxious when the jumps are removed or changed for a special event. Changing the set up of the ring either bi-weekly or as often as possible will help the horse become more welcoming of change.

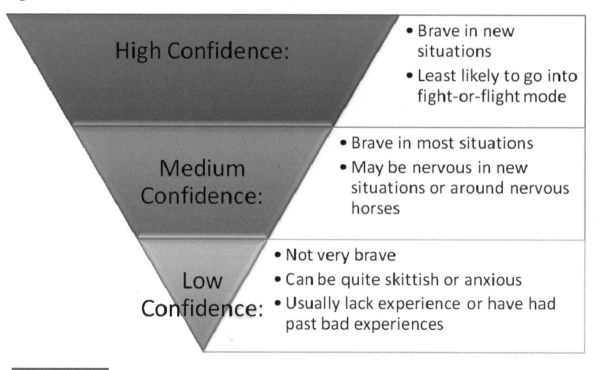

High Confidence:
- Brave in new situations
- Least likely to go into fight-or-flight mode

Medium Confidence:
- Brave in most situations
- May be nervous in new situations or around nervous horses

Low Confidence:
- Not very brave
- Can be quite skittish or anxious
- Usually lack experience or have had past bad experiences

To determine a horse's confidence level, you can assess him quickly by doing three things:

1) Place him in a round pen or small paddock by himself, preferably with no other horses in sight. Is he calm and relaxed with no other horses around?

2) Can he be calm and relaxed in a round pen by himself with you in the pen, but not allowing him within 15 feet of you?

3) When you open an umbrella or shake a plastic bag within 15 feet of the horse but not facing him, does your horse stand still or how far does he move away from it?

If the answer to the above three questions is he stays calm and relaxed, chances are you have a pretty confident horse that is perfect for absolute beginners to work with. If your horse stays calm and relaxed after only a minute or two of being unsettled then this is still a great confidence level, suitable for novices and beginners. If your horse needs a few minutes to settle in these new situations then your horse may require a more intermediate handler. If your horse takes off to the other end of the arena at the site of a plastic bag, or spends over 30 minutes to settle in a round pen, then you likely have a horse that would benefit from an advanced handler and a lot of desensitization exercises. Make sure to change up the environment and introduce new objects like exercise balls, hula-hoops, bells, plastic bags, wind chimes, etc.

Dominance

Have you ever seen a horse threaten to kick as a person approaches his hind end or foot? Many would term this horse aggressive. Often people think being dominant equals being aggressive, but there's a distinct difference between dominance and aggression.

Dominance is innate, whereas aggression is sometimes an expression of trying to be dominant. Aggression can also be a sign of distaste, pain, or fear. For example, when the lead horse tries to move another horse in the field to show he's boss, he may have to bite if that horse doesn't respond to his initial warning signals. This doesn't mean the horse is aggressive, just that he's dominant. Also a horse may try to bite when doing up the girth. This does not mean he is dominant; it could mean he is sore, uncomfortable, or thinking of a past bad experience and thus is responding aggressively.

A submissive horse may show aggression for different reasons, such as trying to bite if the girth hurts when being tightened; or striking out at a person if he feels trapped and/or cornered in a stall or trailer. Submissive horses tend to be picked on in the paddock, and thusly are easily pushed around. They work best with first time beginners and novices, whereas dominant horses are best left for intermediate and advanced level handlers.

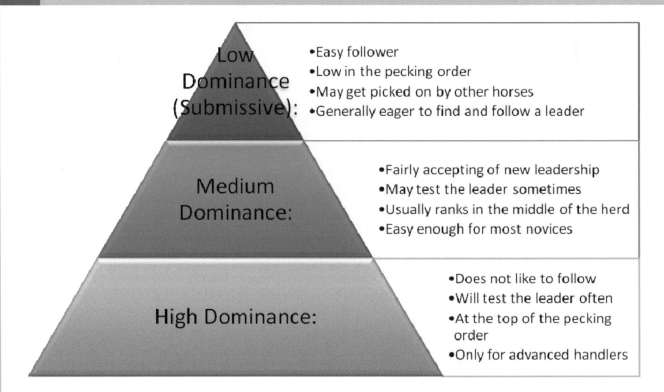

Low Dominance (Submissive):
- Easy follower
- Low in the pecking order
- May get picked on by other horses
- Generally eager to find and follow a leader

Medium Dominance:
- Fairly accepting of new leadership
- May test the leader sometimes
- Usually ranks in the middle of the herd
- Easy enough for most novices

High Dominance:
- Does not like to follow
- Will test the leader often
- At the top of the pecking order
- Only for advanced handlers

Dominance is part of the horse's character; it cannot be modified. Although dominant horses can be taught to follow humans, they will test their leaders more often than submissive horses. Stallions are usually more dominant because they are programmed by nature to be leaders of a herd. They are inclined to prove themselves as leaders, not followers. Stallions are best handled by advanced handlers who can show strong leadership, otherwise the stallion may decide he's a stronger leader and take over for safety's sake—at least the stallion may think your herd of two is safer if he leads. Although some stallions and some dominant horses are quite gentle, well behaved, and can be handled by beginners, if constantly handled by a beginner they may become more dominant in order to fill the leadership need in the partnership.

Dominance can be assessed in two simple ways:

1) When your horse is introduced to a new herd does he stand his ground or move away from the other horses? After a couple of days is he still being pushed around or is he moving other horses around?

2) Are you able to move your horse around easily? Can you back him up, move him forward, and side-to-side? Take notice if resistance is because your cue is unclear, or if the horse is pinning ears/ swishing tail/tensing because he's reluctant to follow you.

If your horse is the type to stay at the bottom of the herd, and is easily moved around, then this is a submissive horse. If the horse is difficult to move around, or threatens to nip or kick when being moved, and is dominant in the herd, then he's a dominant horse. Most horses tend to be somewhere in the middle, and will be happy to follow, providing you show good leadership, though you'll occasionally be tested to ensure you're still a good leader. Testing you makes the horse feel safer if you continue to be a good leader. If you are not an assertive person, or if you do not like correcting horses, then you're best suited to a submissive horse.

Sensitivity

Sensitivity describes how much stimulus is required to get a reaction out of the horse. Sensitivity may start at one level and over time may change to be more or less sensitive. This means that you may have a horse that requires a kick to get moving forward now, but with time and training the horse may move off the slightest leg pressure. If you have a horse that darts forward with the slightest leg pressure, over time with training and good leadership, the horse can be trained to accept more pressure on his side without darting forward. Training will largely determine sensitivity, but it is also innate to some extent.

To test your horse's sensitivity you can check two things:

1) When in a round pen or on a lunge line, what happens if you hit the ground really hard with a whip or stick? (Note: this is quite unfair to the horse, so only do it once to check the horse's response.)

2) When asking for a cue you have done before on the ground, like backing up, moving the front end, or picking up a foot, how much do you have to ask? Do you have to wiggle the rope several times or does just picking up the rope send the horse backwards?

If your horse goes into a short bucking spree or darts forward into a fast pace when you smack the ground while on the lunge, and is quick to respond to a task, then you have a very sensitive horse. These horses are also generally very easy to get going when riding. Horses that just go into a gentle trot when you smack the ground with the whip/stick are likely at a medium level of sensitivity and are good for beginners or novices. Horses that only leave at the walk when on the lunge after hitting the ground may require a more intermediate handler in order to teach them to be more sensitive to cues, but are usually safe for beginners. Beginners may get easily frustrated with a horse with really low sensitivity because although they're asking correctly for something, the horse is not sensitive enough to respond. For example, when I was a beginner I much preferred peppy Peanut when learning to ride, rather than pokey Chuckie.

One fact to remember when testing sensitivity is to realize that a horse may be sensitive, but also dominant. A horse may resist picking up a foot not because the cue is not strong enough, but instead because he's testing your leadership. This is why it's best to test sensitivity by sending a horse out in a round pen, or lunge line, and then smacking the ground rather than by asking for something your horse already knows. However, if you are experienced at reading the horse's

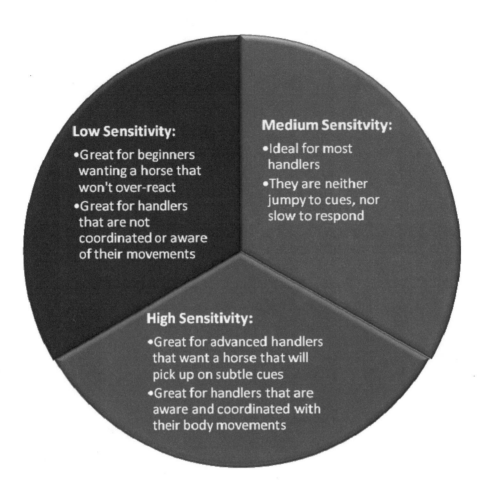

Low Sensitivity:
- Great for beginners wanting a horse that won't over-react
- Great for handlers that are not coordinated or aware of their movements

Medium Sensitvity:
- Ideal for most handlers
- They are neither jumpy to cues, nor slow to respond

High Sensitivity:
- Great for advanced handlers that want a horse that will pick up on subtle cues
- Great for handlers that are aware and coordinated with their body movements

communication signals, then you will be able to tell if resistance is because of dominance, lack of understanding, or lack of sensitivity. Also remember, if you do a task too often, your horse may begin to think he's completing the task incorrectly, so be careful not do overdo a specific task. For example, when backing a horse up, do a few steps at a time and reward the horse by pausing and relaxing after a few steps. If you were to keep asking him to back up, then after six or seven steps the horse may wonder why you're still asking and may decide he's doing it wrongly. He could think you want him to do something else completely and get confused.

Summary

In general, confident, submissive horses with medium sensitivity are best suited to beginners and novices. Horses that lack confidence and are dominant or extremely sensitive are usually best left to advanced handlers. Horses that lack confidence need a handler with a lot of confidence that the horse can draw from—horses can tell when humans are nervous. When you pair a nervous handler with a nervous horse then you have a perfect recipe for something negative to happen.

Note that horses can have different sensitivity levels on the ground versus in the saddle due to past experiences. Horses that were brought up in environments that made them anxious under saddle can mean that the horse is quite sensitive while being ridden, but when handled on the ground the horse can be less sensitive depending on the prior training they received. When this occurs, it is a matter of developing a relationship on the ground and transferring that relationship to the saddle when the horse is ready. If this is done with patience, then over time the sensitivity levels on the ground and in the saddle will become equal.

The best examples I can think of are my experiences with gaited horses. The gaited horses from Pleasure Valley purchased as yearlings with no exposure to the show atmosphere are all calm, relaxed, and none have extreme sensitivity. These were horses purchased from the States and from pedigrees with show history. These horses include Paso Fino, Kentucky Mountain, Tennessee Walkers, Mustangs, etc. and they all have consistent sensitivity levels on the ground as in the saddle. Pleasure Valley's horses compared to many gaited show horses that are trained to ride with no leg at their side, to ride with big bits in their mouths, heads high, etc. tend to have a lot of 'brio' meaning very excited under saddle. These horses with brio could have much lower sensitivity levels under saddle if trained differently from the start. These horses with a lot of brio can be retrained, but it may take a long time depending on how much brio the horse has, the consistency of training, the experience level of the trainer, and how old the horse is.

When purchasing a new horse, I urge you to consider every horse on its own merits and traits, NOT by breed and age alone. Horses have differing levels of confidence, sensitivity and dominance within all breeds and ages of horses. It's unwise to assume that a 15-year-old Quarter Horse, which would typically be a confident and well-tempered horse, will be suitable for a beginner.

I have many examples where I've purchased young horses for beginner and/or nervous students because of the traits the horse possessed. One of my nine-year-old students purchased a four-year-old Quarter Horse mare because she was confident, submissive, and had medium sensitivity, which suited the rider perfectly. They bonded extremely well and several years later are still together. There are many more examples like this. I have also recommended some beginners buy certain Thoroughbreds (typically considered highly sensitive with little confidence) because there are many confident Thoroughbreds with lower sensitivity levels. Many ex-race horses can be successfully trained to be quiet and pokey riding horses, so if an ex-race horse fits your idea for experience, colour and height, then test his character traits to determine if he's right for you.

Mares: to buy or not to buy? Have you heard the old wives' tale that mares are moody and not good for beginners, or that geldings are better tempered than mares? Not true. Some mares can be a little bit 'moody' when in season (in heat). This is because mares know that stallions are on the lookout for them because it's a prime time for breeding, and the mares have to be more protective during this vulnerable time. However, some mares do not change in behaviour at all. Signs of being in season usually include being more sensitive of people and horses around their hind end, urinating more frequently (especially in front of other horses), being more sensitive about horses passing by/

getting too close when working in the ring, or when in the paddock. If their personal space is not respected they may kick or bite.

If you are a good leader for your mare, and your mare considers you trustworthy and is fond of you, then she likely won't be moody. In fact you'll notice when using natural horsemanship a once 'moody' mare may not display moody symptoms any longer. Certain geldings can be just as pushy and moody as some mares. In fact they can be much more dominant if they developed stallion like traits and thus some geldings can be much more of a danger/difficulty to work with than some mares. Personally, I prefer buying mares because I can breed them. Of course, most people will not ever be breeding, so it's best to just find a horse that suits all of your needs.

I always recommend that the gender of the horse be the last thing you consider. Judge every horse on its own merit first—only factor in gender if you have breeding considerations or certain farm conditions that require a certain gender of horse (for example if your farm is not set up to care for a stallion, then you are best not to purchase a stallion).

Criteria to Assess a Horse When Purchasing

1.   Soundness: Is the horse sound for what you want to do? A horse only used for light jumping and flat/trail work does not need the same excellent level of conformation as a horse used for grand prix dressage or jumpers or another discipline that puts excessive strain on the joints. Likewise if you want to breed, you should make sure the horse is breeding sound. If the horse is not able to perform what you want to do then try a different horse. However, make sure not to discount a horse for faults that do not affect the type and/or level of riding you want. For example, a horse with a scar in an eye that affects the vision slightly, but still allows the horse to ride, jump, and trail ride safely, can still have many uses. A horse with pigeon-toed feet (toes that turn inward) may not be suitable for high level jumping because of strain on the front legs, but may be perfect for jumping two-foot courses.

2.   The dominance level you want: Remember, this is innate and not changeable. Training can condition a horse somewhat, but if the horse is consistently handled by someone not matched to his dominance level, problems will arise. If the horse is out of your league, try a different horse.

3.   The confidence level you want: This is hard to change. If you are nervous with horses/riding/ jumping/new situations with horses, then it's important to get a horse that is confident in the area in which you're nervous. Horses can definitely be trained to be more confident, but this can be a time-consuming process, and the horse may require a knowledgeable handler to prevent 'relapse' into becoming a skittish horse again. However, someone who has some horse-savvy may be able to purchase a more timid horse for a bargain price (due to it being more skittish) and still have a very successful relationship.

4. Price: How much can you spend? Do you have a price-range depending on the age and experience a horse has to offer? If you cannot afford a horse with the soundness you need, the dominance level you require, and the confidence level you require then save your money and wait to get a horse best suited to you or you will end up making a mistake. It's heartbreaking to find out you need to sell/replace the horse you purchased and it will cost you more money in the long run.

5. Height, Age range, Breed, and Colour (only if these are important to you): You may want a specific breed to qualify for breed-specific shows or breeding, or you may require a certain height of horse/pony for competition—so depending on the use for the horse, this category may rank higher for you. Remember that horses of all breeds, ages, colour and height can do many things. A 15.2H mare won the jumper height competition at Spruce Meadows a few years ago and a 14.1H pony named Theodore O'Connor won several titles in Eventing against horses who were much bigger. Take into account that a young Thoroughbred can be just as quiet and pokey as an older Quarter Horse.

6. The sensitivity level you want: Keep in mind that if a horse is slightly more pokey or forward than you would like, this can be changed a little bit, but make sure that the horse isn't far from your ideal. Don't buy a naturally slow horse if you prefer more forward horses, and don't buy a forward horse if you prefer a horse that's easy to stop and less sensitive to the 'go button.'

7. The experience and training you want: This can be added to a horse if you have the time for training or the budget to hire a trainer.

8. Gender: Unless you want a mare/stallion for potential breeding, or your paddock/turnout situation requires a mare/gelding, this should be the last thing you consider because mares and geldings can be equally suitable to all disciplines, riders, and levels. More important are the soundness, dominance, confidence, sensitivity, and price of the horse.

Weigh the Pros and Cons of a Horse

THE WHY

Communication and Leadership versus Intimidation and Fear

Have you ever watched the drama of horse-intimidators trying to load a horse onto a trailer? It's unforgettable. Very often in the horse world you will see people cracking a whip at a horse or beating a crop against a horse's shoulder. But you seldom notice the savvy of the horse handler who uses communication and leadership to complete the same tasks because their methods are done in a much calmer and more successful way.

When people witness the relationship that savvy horse handlers have with their horses, they usually think the handlers just got lucky, and managed to buy horses that came with perfect manners. Don't believe it - you can do what they do, and have the relationship with your horse that they have, if you follow natural horsemanship and the principle of communication and leadership rather than fear and intimidation.

The horse-intimidator uses fear and intimidation to force a horse to submit. This leaves horses to guess at the direction and task they are being asked to perform. A horse handler practicing natural horsemanship, using communication and leadership, is able to ask a horse to complete tasks easily and more quickly because the handler understands horse body language and can use this to 'talk' to the horse. The horse in turn understands what is being asked of him and because the leadership that the handler demonstrates is fair, the dignity of the horse is preserved. A horse will willingly follow and accept this kind of handler as a leader. Not only that, the handler will recognize what the horse is saying to them when the horse "disobeys" a task, and react more appropriately.

Horses may disobey a task for many reasons, the most common of which is lack of confidence. Being a fair and trustworthy leader will increase confidence in the horse. Rewarding a horse for trying and asking questions will also increase confidence in the horse. Contrarily, a horse that is often punished will get nervous about trying new things and offering new things to a rider in fear of being punished for the wrong attempt.

There are many reasons why we should use communication and leadership when working with horses rather than intimidation and fear. When you demonstrate strong leadership, you fill a natural need the horse is born with. As prey animals, horses are primarily concerned with being safe. When you demonstrate strong leadership, your horse feels safe and will **want** to follow you and cooperate with you. When you build a language together through non-verbal and verbal cues, it allows you to communicate and have an understanding with the horse. This understanding makes teaching new concepts, handling and riding much easier.

Natural horsemanship builds a relationship of trust, respect, and ultimately a functional relationship in which the handler can get desired results from the horse without theatrical performances, and in a much more effective way than the intimidator's technique.

Intimidation and fear are typically the traditional form of training used with horses. This technique focuses on bullying a horse into submission and forcing the horse to perform. The horse loses dignity, trust and respect for the handler during this process and the relationship is severely damaged. This technique suffers from several key elements to success with horses.

The three important reasons to avoid using intimidation and fear as a method of training are:

Frame of Mind: A horse functions on one of two planes of thought. The horse can be in a thinking frame of mind, which means the horse is using his brain and can logically work through tasks and can be focused and perceptive to stimuli around him. A horse in this frame of mind is open to cues from the handler, and is able to perform tasks. The second frame of mind is one of fight-or-flight. This is a primitive response to a fearful or threatening situation.

A common example is when a horse refuses a jump in the show ring. The rider then tries to intimidate the horse or instill fear by whipping him with a crop either once or several times. When the rider does this, the horse turns to fight-or-flight mode, and often you'll see the horse buck or rear, or when turned at the jump to retake the fence, speed towards or after it to try and run. The horse is running because of fear, and running from the rider. Now the rider has a horse that is not in a thinking frame of mind and is unlikely to be receptive to cues and new tasks. This is a poor frame of mind when working with horses, and even worse when in competition, which requires the horse's full attention.

Provoking dangerous behaviour: Based on the example above, in a similar situation, when faced with a new fence to jump, or an unsure circumstance, the horse is likely to remember the cropping and will speed towards/after jumps, may start bucking after jumps or may begin stopping dirty (refuses the fence and intentionally tries to toss the rider off his back). This is all to avoid cropping.

This is dangerous behaviour and is one of the ways in which people can be harmed when working with horses. Another example is when a horse is put into a new situation and appears "hot," meaning the horse is tense, keeps moving, is alert, may be calling or nickering to friends, and may be moving quickly. If the handler were a source of comfort and had a good relationship with the horse this would likely not be happening at all, but what can make matters worse is when handlers hit or bully the horse for being scared and unsure. This only serves to make the horse more scared and more unsure. In addition to making the horse more upset, the relationship between human and horse is severely damaged. This means that if you're trail riding and try to kick your horse past a fallen log or barking dog, you are more likely to have your horse take off than you are to have him walk calmly and confidently. Or if you were to fall off, your horse is more likely to run away from you rather than stand by your side.

The will to please: Even more detrimental than the frame of mind and provoking dangerous behaviour is the loss of the will to please. Because of excessive cropping or intimidation, the horse loses the will to please and perform for the handler. The horse may oblige a rider by jumping a fence or performing a task, but it is just amazing what horses can do when they use their full potential, which can only be mastered when your horse *wants* to work for you.

Your horse will only want to work for you if you have a relationship that preserves his dignity and allows for trust and respect. When you have a positive relationship, your horse will start to offer things to you. For example, while practicing collected canter circles with my five-year-old Thoroughbred, she offered canter pirouette, which is an upper level dressage move that usually takes months or years of training to achieve. She offered this to me with less than 10 rides together - after coming straight off the race track and being a chestnut mare to boot!

Horses who want to please you will offer flying lead changes at the canter, will put in the extra effort to clear the fences or make the fastest time, and perform the best piaffe. There is a big difference between getting a clear round in a jump off and achieving a clear round with the fastest time because the horse was fully focused on pleasing you rather than swishing his tail in protest. This is the difference that communication and leadership offer.

Horses are amazing animals with a natural way of communicating with humans and each other. Horses are more than willing to follow as long as you can prove to be a strong leader who is fair, trustworthy and can keep them safe. Once you establish yourself as a worthy leader your horse will try his best to please you.

You can start with basic cues. These will be the foundation to a language spoken through your movements. It evolves and develops as you play with your horse. Using your imagination, you can think up new puzzles for your horse to solve and have a clear picture of what you would like your horse to perform.

Having a focus is key to leading a horse because if there is no goal in mind then there is no goal at all. Your horse needs to know what you are asking and also needs to know when he has met that task. Preserving your horse's dignity will preserve the will of your horse making the two of you a strong team that will be a success on a trail or a force to be reckoned with in the show ring.

Natural horsemanship concepts can be applied to horses of all breeds, ages, heights, and genders, participating in all disciplines at all levels with any type of rider. ***There is no excuse for abuse***. Patience and time will be great factors in your success as will support from appropriate people. Being confident in your decision to practice naturally will play a major role in your journey with natural horsemanship and how far you can go.

Having humility and seeking help when you face challenges beyond your comprehension are a must. Horses forgive and horses can learn new tricks.

Opening the door to natural horsemanship is opening a door with many possibilities, surprises, and a whole new positive way of working with horses in a safer, more meaningful, and more connected way. You need only to ask yourself one question: are you ready for change?

The Environment

Often people who practice natural horsemanship will also advocate for a natural environment such as pasture or outdoor boarding. Outdoor boarding means a horse is kept outside twenty-four hours a day and seven days a week except when being worked, or being brought in for a feeding or other form of care. The horse does not spend extended periods of time in a stall. There is always access to water in the field and the field has proper shelter for shade, rain and snow. The field needs to be appropriate to mentally keep the horse healthy such as having field mates and enough space to graze, or perhaps a jolly ball or other interesting objects to check out if the paddock is too small to have naturally occurring objects like logs, trees, streams, ditches, hills, and/or other animals.

Many outdoor boarding facilities will give continuous access to hay or grass, a mineral salt lick or supplement, and may provide supplemental feedings. Outdoor board horses may or may not be blanketed. Turnout of horses is best when there are more than two horses so they can play together and fill social needs such as grooming each other, challenging each another, and establishing rank. If a horse has one other field mate, then the dominant horse can become exceptionally dominant because he/she is seldom challenged. That means a lot of extra work for the handler to really prove to the horse that he/she is the dominant leader.

Fields can be a mix of mares and geldings. However, when mixing mares and geldings, sometimes the males can become protective or really attached to their mares. This depends on the horses' characters. Separating mares and geldings or mixing genders can be beneficial. Turning a stallion out with geldings can be excellent for their mental health as long as they have appropriate paddock mates. Never turn a stallion out with a mare unless you want the mare to become pregnant. Be sure to monitor the stallion because he may chase the mare if he wants to breed, even if the mare is not ready.

Outdoor versus Indoor Board

Many people like to stall their horses, especially those who compete. The reasons for indoor boarding (stalling horses) may include: to keep their horses safe, convenient for catching, working, and feeding, and to keep a watchful eye on them. However, you should consider the healthiest choice for your horse and put your own feelings aside if you truly want what is best for your horse. When planning a turnout routine, remember that horses sleep only an average of three to four hours per day. If you bring your horse in at 5 pm, and do not turn out your horse until 7 am the next morning, he is standing in a stall—usually a space of approximately 10 feet by 10 feet for over 10 waking hours, doing nothing. If the horse doesn't have enough hay to last the time in the stall, he'll become incredibly bored and may develop vices.

Vices are bad habits picked up that simulate natural needs. Examples include wind sucking and cribbing, which involves the horse biting down with the front teeth. Horses perform these vices to fulfill the need of grazing; it's easily prevented when adequate turnout is provided. Stall walking and pacing fulfill the need of movement; shifting from leg to leg stimulates blood flow. Excessive stalling causes these problems.

Horses may become pushy, aggressive, and in general grumpier (pinning ears when people walk by and showing general displeasure when at work) when excessively stalled. Because of the size of the stalls, it means that each horse continuously has another horse in his personal space (10 feet). Horses will often stand as far away as possible from other horses unless they are directly interacting. They become pushy and aggressive because their social needs to play, challenge, and perform the ritual of determining rank cannot be fulfilled in a stall. This is also why individual turnout is not recommended unless the horse is injured, ill, or at a high risk for injury and no safe paddock mate is available for companion turnout.

Therefore **the more turnout you can provide to your horse, the better**. If you are worried about injury to your horse, then it is recommended that you provide a small paddock and safe paddock mate—such as an older submissive horse, a goat, or donkey.

People often question outdoor board because horses so willingly enter their stalls, and because they feel sorry for horses that are outside during bad weather. Have you ever noticed that usually when horses are put in a stall there is grain waiting for them, or grain arrives shortly? Try putting a horse in a stall without food—how happy and eager is he to go in when there is no food? And remember that most of the time spent in the stall the horses don't have food because it takes them only minutes to eat grain and an hour or two to eat a flake of hay. Ever notice that outdoor paddocks have easily enough space for all the horses in the field (at least a space of 10 feet x 10 feet per horse)? Also notice that despite roomy run in shelters, during rain and snow most horses choose to be outside?

Some farms may not be set up properly for outdoor board. Horses need roomy shelters with enough space for all horses, areas for shade, water, hay, and flat dry footing. Icy, really hard, or really muddy footing is not good for horses over long periods of time and stalls do provide rest from these harsh footings, but so can adequate shelter if available.

Horses need to have an area of flat, dry, soft ground to cushion the feet, prevent mud fever, and be helpful to the joints and positioning. It is important that horses have adequate shelter and that all the horses can access the shelter in order to prevent heat stroke from too much sun, rain rot from too much rain, or colds from getting too wet from rain and then too cool from a cold night. Generally horses will take care of themselves and will not put themselves into situations where they will make themselves sick when provided with adequate shelter, but a horse cannot benefit from shade on a hot day if it's not provided.

Horses can also benefit from some time in mud or on hard ground. Mud moistens the hoof and helps prevent cracking. Hard surfaces help the hoof to develop calluses and sturdy hooves. Pressure within the hoof prevents thrush (a hoof disease of the frog, a part of the hoof that starts to rot when inadequate pressure is exerted on it). This happens more often in the spring when horses are mostly on really soft ground. Hard ground also provides some natural wear so the horse needs trimming less often.

Outdoor horses require monitoring to ensure their safety and health. They require good grooming and overall inspection to check for skin conditions, scrapes, or infection—especially in the particularly wet and muddy seasons. Be careful to monitor the available grass or hay within the paddock because the requirements will change with the seasons.

Proper nutrition for horses begins with quality forage. Having good hay and pasture can eliminate the need for nutritional supplements in a horse's diet. Forage plays a major role in the horse's diet and can yield a large amount of nutritional value, so grazing time should not be under-valued.

Amy Gill, PhD, an equine nutritionist based in Lexington, Kentucky, advocates a nutritional plan for a horse by starting with hay or pasture, and then adding grain concentrates and supplements only as needed. All you need to provide is salt and fresh water if you have proper forage. However, if forage is not ideal, or if your horse is stabled, then you should add a supplement containing protein, vitamins, and minerals. If your horses don't have access to pasture then you've limited the horse to what you provide.

Much research has been done comparing domestic horses to wild horses and it is well documented that wild horses live on average 10 to 20 years longer than domestic horses kept in stalls. Outdoor board horses also tend to live longer than stalled horses. Research is ongoing and we continuously learn more about the horse's natural environment, nutrition, and hoof care.

Being outside with ample space and field mates (other horses) allows a horse to satisfy the social part of his brain. This can serve for a couple of purposes:

1) The horse can fulfill its desire to play with other horses, and can also learn manners and communication with other horses so they are not pushy around humans.

2) Their minds will be more active so they do not develop vices such as cribbing or weaving.

Being outside with ample space and field mates also has physical benefits. Walking around to graze helps a horse in two major ways:

1)   Continuous walking helps fill the hoof with new blood as the hoof expands with each step, making the hoof grow stronger. If you shoe or stall your horse then you prevent this from happening.

2) Continuous grazing is healthier for the horse's teeth and stomach, which were designed for more continuous eating in small frequent meals, rather than large meals three to four times per day.

Going Barefoot

There has been a lot of research in the last few years related to natural barefoot trimming and natural horse shoeing.

Keeping a horse barefoot, especially a competition horse has been a topic of debate amongst many horse professionals. Natural Hoof Trimmers are on the rise, and require a certification program that focuses on how the hoof works naturally in the wild and how we can help our horses to have the best hoof health, which ultimately affects the horse's overall health.

There are three main criteria to keep a horse's hooves healthy in addition to a regular trim. They are:

1. **Movement**: Constant movement provides blood flow to nourish the hoof and allows for natural exfoliation. This is one of the reasons why plenty of turnout, preferably 24/7 turnout, is recommended.

2. **Moisture**: Moisture can come in many forms, including morning dew, snow, or mud. In dry summers you can hose the area in front of the water trough so that the horses have to step in mud/water to get a drink. This helps the hooves stay flexible so there is minimal chipping and cracking.

3. **A Well Balanced Diet**: Horses, just like humans, require a mixture of vitamins and minerals to allow for proper function and growth. Horses obtain 80% of moisture for their hooves from internal sources, only 20% comes from environment.

Having shoes on your horse can predispose your horse to other ailments. Nail holes in the hooves can cause abscesses, infections and potentially more harmful effects. Shoes can also put your horse at risk for hurting other horses out in the paddock. More damage is done with a kick from a hoof with a shoe than one without. Horses can even rip the shoe and hoof right off if the horse overreaches with the hind leg and catches the back of the front horse shoe, or even just from getting stuck in deep mud. Shoes also ball snow within the hoof during the snowy months and create 'horse ice skates' for the horse to walk on—very dangerous. If your horse has shoes in the snowy months, make sure the horse has snow pads to prevent the balling of snow.

If you currently shoe your horse or are thinking about shoeing your horse, you should consider carefully if the horse really requires shoes for his job and well-being. For further information contact a natural hoof care/barefoot specialist near you.

Keeping it Natural

1. Jen demonstrates a strong bond with Rain **2, 3,** & **4.** A natural environment for your horse keeps them healthy **5.** Swimming with your horse means a trusting relationship **6.** Allowing your horse to be curious can do wonders for your relationship

1.

4.

5.

2.

6.

3.

The Tools

You can recognize a natural horseman by the tools they will use and the tools they won't use. You can also recognize a natural horseman by *how* they use their tools.

There are many different tools you can use with your horse in a natural way, and some are better than others. There are also tools that are generally considered natural and fair but used in the wrong way can be just as harmful and unnatural as other tools.

The Halter

Many natural horsemanship users advocate rope halters. This is because the knots of the rope sit near facial nerves, which more clearly distribute pressure. This makes communication more clear to the horse.

However, because the knots sit near facial nerves, a horse should never be tied when in a rope halter unless the horse has already been taught to give to pressure, and is supervised. Otherwise, if a horse panics while tied and wearing a rope halter there is greater chance for nerve injury than with an ordinary nylon or leather halter, which distributes pressure evenly. For example, when trailering your horse it is recommended to tie a horse using a leather halter for the journey—this type of halter will break under high pressure and thus there will be minimal damage to the horse.

The standard nylon and leather halters distribute pressure too evenly, which makes it difficult to communicate clearly with your horse. The thicker the halter, the more comfortable it is, and the easier it is for a horse to ignore pressure or to be confused as to whether you are asking for something or not.

In order for a horse to yield to pressure, it must be very clear what is comfortable and what is uncomfortable (this does not mean painful), so when you release the tension from a rope halter there is greater reward than from releasing tension from a regular leather or nylon halter. Also, when you pull on a rope halter, the knots clearly put pressure on specific points on the horse's head and more clearly communicate which direction you want the head to move.

The Lead Rope

The longer and denser the rope is the better. You are safest when you can control your horse from farther than an arm's length away. The more distance you put in-between you and your horse, the safer you are. This is why working with a loose horse in a round pen (60 feet in diameter or greater) is the safest way to assess a new horse, or to join up with a new horse.

You also show better leadership when you can direct the horse without touching him, and when you keep your personal space clear. As mentioned earlier, your personal space is a 10 foot bubble of space around you, not just an arm's length. For this reason a rope of 12 feet or longer is recommended. As you become more familiar with maneuvering your horse, and handling your rope, you can extend your rope to longer lengths.

Starting with a 10 to 12 foot rope will help you to become organized with your cues and handling of your tools before you progress to longer ropes such as 20 to 25 feet for intermediate levels, and up to 50 feet in advanced levels.

It is important for the rope to be a dense material so that it has 'feel' in it. If you wiggle the rope, the movement should carry to the other end of the rope and not get lost along the way. A yacht rope 2-3 centimeters in diameter is a good choice. Be sure to get a rope that is both thick and dense. There are many cotton lead ropes available that are thick, but very light and thus not as useful when communicating with horses.

To test the feel in your rope: have someone hold one end of the rope, and you hold the other. Give the rope a **gentle** wiggle (movement only from your wrist) and determine if the wiggle can make it down the rope. If the rope is too stiff or too light then the wiggle in the rope will not make it to the other end. When doing this exercise be sure that the rope is not touching the ground or other objects that may interfere.

The rope should also have a heavy snap at the end. This is to have better communication with the horse. Ropes that tie directly to the halter without a metal snap are NOT the best when training a horse and teaching new skills—they are better suited to horses that already have a good understanding of the basics, with medium or higher levels of sensitivity. This is for two reasons: The first is because you may have to give your rope a hard wiggle and get the metal snap to tag the horse under the chin to get the horse's attention. This is not to cause pain to the horse, but to be safe by giving you the option to use a higher intensity cue if needed. Just because a rope has a metal snap on the end does not mean that you will use the snap to bite the horse, but as a 'backup' measure it is essential to have with new horses, when teaching new skills, and with less sensitive horses. The second reason is because the heavy snap adds weight to the rope, which will allow the horse to feel even the slightest movement of the rope more clearly.

The Bridle or Hackamore

How often have you seen a fast horse forced to wear a stronger bit? Would you be surprised to learn that horses are better started without a bit in the mouth at all, and are best started in a rope hackamore or a side-pull? This takes what you do on the ground and moves it to the saddle.

Bits are used for advanced communication once you have permission to be in your horse's mouth. A bit is not needed until you are ready to advance beyond the cues of go, stop, turn right, turn left, and back up in the saddle. You should not use a noseband when introducing the bit. When the horse opens his mouth with a bit inside, it means there is too much pressure in the mouth. When you tie the mouth shut you are not allowing the horse to communicate with you—this damages the relationship.

Some people say you need a noseband because if the horse avoids the pressure of the bit you can lose control. However, when a horse does this, you can still effectively stop the horse with one rein by doing an emergency stop (explained later). You're unlikely to have this problem anyway if you take the natural approach and start your horse with a hackamore, then ride with both a hackamore and a bridle with bit. Only after several rides with both the hackamore and the bridle with the bit, you can then safely switch to just the bridle with the bit.

If the horse isn't giving you the answer you want when you pull back on his mouth, then you need to assess your relationship, leadership, respect, and readiness for a bit. A problem in the saddle is always related to a problem on the ground.

Your horse should never require a harsh bit, and you should never think 'I can't stop my horse, so I am going to get a more severe bit.' Instead consider why your horse doesn't want to stop. Usually it is fear or a lack of respect. These are bigger issues that should be addressed, rather than a band-aid solution of getting a stronger bit.

There is no need for nosebands at all; however, some competitions require a noseband as a preventative measure in case the horse tries to avoid the bit during competition. In this case, a basic noseband/cavesson should be used on a loose setting to meet competition requirements. If your horse is avoiding pressure on the bit then you need to assess why. It could be readiness for the bit, improper size of bit, wrong type of bit for your horse, or lack of readiness for the situation/ environment you are in.

All of these factors should be addressed individually, rather than just tying your horse's mouth shut. When the horse opens his mouth while a bit is in, he's communicating with you that something is not right, that the pressure is too much. You should listen to the horse, not shut him up.

If your horse is being introduced to the bit, or is not ready to be ridden in bridle and bit, then ride with both a rope hackamore and bridle. This means you will have two sets of reins. One set of reins will be attached to the rope hackamore; the second set of reins will be attached to the bit. At first, ride your horse without even touching the reins attached to the bit. After a couple of rides doing that, you can pick up both sets of reins and ride with both. Once your horse is comfortable, you can start riding with just the reins that are attached to the bit, and leave the reins attached to the rope hackamore hanging over the neck or horn of the saddle as back up if the horse gets confused or resists. After a few successful rides use the reins attached to the bit only, with the rope hackamore also on as a backup, until you are ready to use just the bridle with the bit and thus only one set of reins.

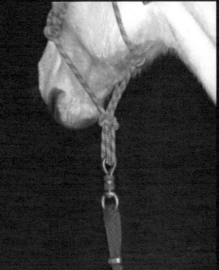

Top Left: a bitless bridle

Top Centre: a rope halter with a lead with a heavy snap

Top Right: a rope halter with double knots across the nose

Left Centre: a horse wearing both a rope hackamore and a bridle with a bit over top (for teaching a horse to accept the bit you wear both the hackamore and bridle)

Left: arm extension stick with string

When choosing a bit, choose one that is appropriate to the horse's mouth size, and that will not easily be pulled through the horse's mouth. My favourite choice is a happy mouth, large D-ring, with a French link. This means the bit has soft plastic around the metal, has large D-rings on either side of the horses mouth that keep the bit stable within the mouth, and a French link is a flat piece in the middle of the bit that sits flat across the horse's tongue. The flat piece over the tongue means that when the rider pulls on the bit, the bit does not fold and press into the roof of the horse's mouth. Instead the flat piece across the tongue acts as the communication, causing no pain. Although this is my preference, I must always choose a bit that is best suited to the horse. Some horses do best with bits that have rollers, rubber, or copper.

Crops, Whips, Spurs, and Sticks

Many natural horsemanship users will use a stick or some form of extension of their arm or leg. This is simply because having an extension of your arm or leg gives you more reach; it can make up for weak legs/arms, and also can give you more confidence. For example, when asserting your dominance and touching a horse all over, you may not want to rub a horse on the belly with your hand because you may be worried about getting hurt if the horse reacts negatively.

When using a stick you can rub the horse and stay at a safe distance; this gives you the confidence you need to complete the task. Sometimes riders may have weaker legs, so a rounded soft spur may be needed to help their leg because the rider tires easily, but should never be used to inflict pain or to be used to intimidate the horse. Some riders who ride several horses a day will use a crop or spurs for the same reason, but remember it's unwise to use a spur with the intent to cause pain.

Crops can be humane if used only as an extension of the leg or hand and not as a beating or punishing tool. The goal of natural horsemanship is communication, not intimidation or to inflict pain. Some riders may use a piece of rope rather than a crop because it is more easily exchanged from side to side, and has more feel and softness to it.

Saddles and Pads

Every discipline requires its own saddle, and the saddle must suit the needs of the rider as well as the horse. However, when fitting a saddle, make sure the saddle suits your horse because an ill-fitting saddle cannot be corrected with saddle pads to prevent pinching or pain if the structure of the saddle itself does not fit the horse.

The saddle pad's main purpose is to protect the saddle from sweat. It can also make the saddle sit more comfortably and lessen the chance of rubs. Pads that are too thick can actually make a saddle more uncomfortable for the horse depending on the shape of the saddle and the pressure exerted on the horse's spine.

Checking for a level saddle

Checking for wither clearance

Different saddle pad thicknesses

Checking for wither clearance

Using a crop to check for clearance along the horse's back

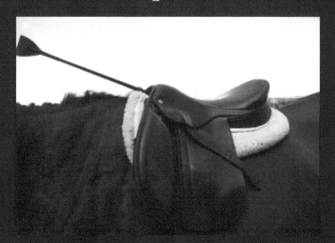

Checking for a level saddle

The saddle pad can also help to raise a saddle up off the withers of the horse to ensure clearance along the top line of the horse (the saddle should not sit on any of the bones along the back (the spine) of the horse). Many western saddle pads can come with a thicker front, known as a 'built up' pad, or a 'front riser' pad to serve this purpose.

Most risers or wither relief pads meant for English saddles are separate pads that are put over top of the basic saddle blanket. Some riders may use gel pads to help absorb shock from a rider bouncing on the horse's back, or from jumping. In any case, be sure that your padding does not interfere with the movement of the horse's shoulder, and that there is still clearance between the saddle and the horse's spine (you should be able to easily stick a crop through the gullet of the saddle).

When using any pad under a saddle, make sure you have a 'saddle pad poof' as follows: Place the saddle pad on your horse's back as usual. Then place the saddle over top of the pad. Before you do up the girth, pull the saddle pad up into the gullet/pommel area of the saddle. This will create a 'saddle pad poof' in that the saddle pad will be off of the horse's withers, and instead be pushed up into the saddle so that it touches the inner side of the saddle side.

To understand the importance of a 'saddle pad poof', place your saddle pad and saddle on without doing the poof. Then do up the saddle as usual, and sit on the horse's back. Try to fit your finger between the saddle pad and the horse's withers. It's practically impossible and very tight against the horse's back. This creates of a lot of pressure and can cause soreness to the horse making your horse reluctant to round their top line and collect properly.

Common Saddle Fitting Faults

1)   Sitting the saddle too far forward—many people love to put their saddle as far forward as possible in fear of being behind the motion of the horse. Putting a saddle too far forward on a horse can block the movement in the shoulder and impair the horse's movement, or can bring about pain, causing the horse to move differently. This can make the horse's muscle to reshape and move in an unnatural way. However, if the saddle is too far back, it could cause back pain if it is not supported by weight bearing ribs. Just like humans, horses have a large set of weight bearing ribs that can hold weight, and also some floating ribs that cannot bear weight. To check the proper saddle position, follow these simple steps:

1.   Place the saddle on the horse's back.

2.   Feel for the end of the shoulder blade and put the saddle behind the end of the shoulder blade.

3.   Pick up one of the horse's front legs and hold it out in front of you. Now feel the difference in the shoulder blade and push the saddle behind the movement in the shoulder.

4. Check that the saddle is level and clearing the withers completely. Saddles that are positioned so they are tilting downward need a saddle pad with extra padding at the front to bring the saddle level. Over time with exercise the muscles may change and saddle stuffing and positioning will need to be reassessed.

5. Check that the saddle does not sit beyond the last weight bearing rib. To feel for the last weight bearing rib, run your hand down the horse's side and when you feel a drop after the last rib, you have passed the last weight bearing rib.

6. Follow the last weight bearing rib up to the spine and be sure the saddle does not go beyond that rib.

7. Do up the girth.

8. Sit in the saddle. Double check that the withers are still cleared by at least 1 centimeter by the saddle. Make sure you can feel the back of the shoulder blade.

9. Warm up the horse in walk and trot.

10. Check the saddle again for clearance between the saddle and the withers/top line of the horse.

11. After a ride with your horse that causes the horse to sweat, remove the saddle and check for even sweat marks from the saddle. If there is an area that is not sweaty, it is likely the saddle is not making as much contact with that particular spot and the saddle fit may need to be adjusted.

To feel how painful a saddle can be when positioned incorrectly, put the saddle on slightly too far forward (for some this may be your usual saddle position, which you will need to change). Then feel for the back of the shoulder (with or without anyone sitting in the saddle, but be sure the saddle is secure and girth tightened).

Walk the horse forward while still leaving your hand by the shoulder. Feel the pinching? Now imagine how much worse it is at the canter, or when landing from a jump. If there is no rider in the saddle, then imagine the difference with the weight of a rider on the horse's back.

Properly positioning the saddle can correct many problems such as bucking at the canter, bucking after jumps, head tossing going into the canter and during the canter, tense canter, reluctance to round the top line, and excessive swishing of the tail that are sometimes mistaken as behavioural problems. Horses that continually have saddles placed too far forward may need frequent massages to relieve muscle knots in the back and shoulders and may be prone to pressure sores on the withers and back.

2)   Having a saddle that is too big for the horse's back - this is most commonly seen in horses with short backs and with ponies. Sometimes a rider requires a bigger saddle for their own needs such as a 16" to 18" saddle. When placed on a horse with a shorter back or a pony, it can place extra strain on the back muscles, and the muscles over the hind end of the horse will have to compensate. The muscle group often affected with this type of situation appears like a bump over the croup along the horse's top line. If your horse has a firm bump of muscle on their back near the croup, it is most likely because of the saddle being too big.

Ill-fitting saddles overtime may cause the horse to develop muscles to counteract the strain, which can hinder their performance. If you suspect an ill-fitting saddle, or can feel muscle knots/bumps along your horse's back or top line, have your saddle assessed immediately for fitting before serious damage occurs. Equine chiropractors are generally excellent to consult about saddle fit and they can provide insight into your horse's alignment and any stiffness present. Massage therapy can help to loosen muscle knots in the horse once the saddle fit has been corrected.

If you do not correct the saddle fit, the muscle knots and spinal misalignments will keep coming back. It is important not to loosen the knots in the horse with massage and then continue to ride in the ill-fitting saddle. This is because the muscle knots are there from protecting the horse's back from the ill-fitting saddle. Removing the muscle knots may improve stiffness and movement but will also take away the back's protection created from the stiff knots. Make sure to stop using an ill-fitting saddle immediately, especially after you start treatment.

Failing to get rid of muscle knots can strain the horse's spine and cause misalignment of the bones, requiring a chiropractor. Failure to realign the bones can impair movement and damage the nervous system, which affects all aspects of your horse's health. Misalignments can cause headaches, poor vision, weakened organ function, stiff joints, and other problems. Having regular adjustments to keep the spine in line is essential during the treatment phase, and maintenance adjustments may be needed semi-annually in order to keep the spine in line during the maintenance phase.

Important Things to Check When Fitting the Saddle

1.   Let there be light! Make sure there is an enough space between the wither/spine/back and the pommel/gullet/saddle so that you can see light, or take a crop and make sure you can pass it easily between the horse and the saddle along the spine of the horse. Double check this after you sit on the horse, and after you do a warm up because saddle position shifts as you ride.

2.   Check that the angle of the saddle matches the angle of the horse's back. Add stuffing if required to shape the saddle, and be sure to have the right tree size to allow for the proper angle (the tree is like the spine of the saddle and maintains the shape and support inside

the saddle). For example: If the horse has a narrow v-shaped back, then your saddle should have the same narrow v-angle as the horse. To help purchase a saddle in store, take a wire hanger and bend it over your horse's withers so that it makes contact with the horse's back at every spot on the hanger. Once shaped, remove the wire and trace the angle on a piece of paper. Take the piece of paper and hanger with you to the tack shop. You may have to line up your hanger with the piece of paper to reshape the hanger if it gets bent out of shape on the way to the tack shop. Using the hanger you can see if the angle of the saddle will match the angle of your horse without even taking the saddle home!

3. Make sure the saddle sits straight and is not tipping forward or backward. You may require a special pad to raise the front of the saddle or lift the back end to make sure the seat of the saddle is level. Otherwise too much pressure can be exerted on one area on the back. Saddles usually have buckles, snaps, screws, or decoration that can help you determine if the saddle is tilted. When the saddle is on a level saddle rack, look to see if the pieces of hardware on the saddle line up, and are level on the saddle (one piece should be near the front and one near the back of the saddle). Then place the saddle on the horse—are the two pieces of hardware still lined up? Adjust padding until the saddle is level.

THE HOW

The Seven Principles

When using natural horsemanship, you must consider the seven basic principles of natural horsemanship:

1) **The goal is communication, not intimidation**. When working with horses you should always be thinking about what your body language and cues are saying to the horse and what the horse is saying to you. The ideal is to communicate with your horse in terms of cues, and realize how body movements mean different things. For example, if you can teach a horse to move away from pressure (i.e. if you want a horse to move over you press his side and release the pressure when he moves) then you can expand on that basic communication to mean that anytime the horse feels pressure, he should move away from it. You should be able to pull on the horse's tail and he should give to the pressure by following the feel through the tail. Another example: when riding, add the slightest pressure on the mouth which is pressure in front of the horse, so the horse stops and/or backs up.

   You need consistent language that you can repeat, reuse, and build on. Every time you apply pressure in a certain way, it should be specific to the action you want, and should be a cue that is logical to the horse. This allows you to participate in many more disciplines, tricks, or games you can play with horses because you can fine tune your body language to avoid confusion.

   Another example is when using a crop as a communication tool you can ask a horse to yield the forehand, hindquarters, or to move more forward but when used as a beating stick to punish the horse and beat him into submission, you lose that communication piece. When used to punish the horse, the crop becomes something that produces only negative effects and provokes a horse to buck, swish the tail, get quick, and lose respect for the rider.

2) **The leader's space takes priority**. This translates into meaning that the leader can move whomever he wants in the herd; the leader can touch whomever he wants in the herd; the leader will protect the space of his followers and himself; and the leader will not move out of the way for anyone, any horse, or any other animal.

   The leader's space is to be respected, and the leader will protect the followers in their space. This respect comes with responsibility. The leader must protect the space of his followers. If you are leading a horse out of a paddock and he gets kicked by a different horse on the way out of the gate, he can no longer trust you as a safe leader.

   You can observe this in the paddock. When you introduce a new horse to a herd you will see a pecking order established. The horse at the top of the pecking order is easily identified because he stands his ground, moves the other horses, touches the other horses, and goes wherever he wants. If you are unsure who the herd boss is, you can often observe pecking orders during feeding because the herd boss will get the first pile of food, and is able to move submissive horses away from their food if he wants it.

3) **Start with your ideal cue.** Always start with your ideal cue and then ask fairly, ask gently, ask firmly, and reward greatly when you get the correct answer. Follow this progression when asking your horse something so that he understands that you are consistent and fair in your approach. As a result, your horse will start to be more aware of your ideal cues and react to them appropriately. This also follows the premise that it is comfortable to do the right thing and uncomfortable to do the wrong thing. By starting with your ideal cue and then increasing the intensity of the cue, you help your horse realize what you want by making the correct response comfortable and the wrong response progressively more uncomfortable. For example asking a horse to go forward while riding with a soft squeeze of the leg, and then increase intensity to a firm squeeze, then a soft kick, then finally a gentle tap of a crop or a swing of a rope behind the leg if the horse has not yet moved forward. As soon as the horse moves forward you relax your leg and become a passenger.

When observing horses in their herd, you will notice that the herd boss will always ask gently first when he wants a horse to move. He will pin his ears, move intently, open the mouth threatening to bite, raise a leg threatening to kick, and if the horse he wishes to move has not gotten the hint, or wishes to challenge the herd boss, then the herd boss will ask firmly which may include a bite or a kick.

After the horse moves away, the herd boss will reward greatly by leaving the horse completely alone, or may even allow the horse to follow or rejoin the herd. It is very uncommon for a horse to chase another horse in an aggressive manner unless the horse is being dangerous to the herd, or threatening the leader in the herd (such as a new horse or another stallion).

When a paddock is too small to accommodate the number of horses in the herd, a new horse, or a horse not considered part of the herd, may be chased because the field is not large enough for the unaccepted horse to leave the space of the herd. Small paddocks can have large numbers if the horses all get along and are considered part of the herd—equal access to shelter, hay and water must be provided.

4) **The reward is in the release.** Remember that when you stop asking, it must be because the horse was correct, not because you gave up. Therefore if you are asking your horse to pick up a hoof, and he kicks at you, and as a result you stand up scared and step back, then the horse thinks he must have reacted correctly because you rewarded him by leaving him alone. This is so important—failure to remember this principle is usually the root cause for much 'misbehaviour'.

Other examples include people asking a slow horse to go forward, and then when the horse doesn't, in frustration they stop asking and sit in the saddle, frustrated. The horse naturally assumes 'this must be some desensitizing exercise' (meaning the horse thinks you are trying to teach him to tolerate flapping legs on his sides—such as when we practice desensitizing games with our horses, when using fly spray, bathing, clipping, saddling, etc.). Then the next time you ask the horse to go forward, he continues to ignore you. If you are asking something of a horse, continue asking until you get the answer you want and then reward IMMEDIATELY by releasing any pressure/cue (stop asking and stand/sit there).

Similarly, when you ask a horse to stop by pulling back on the reins, you must release the pressure on the reins when he slows/stops, to signal that he's reacted correctly. Be careful that what you are asking is the most clear way, and that it is fair and holds realistic expectations for the horse based on age, training, fitness, confidence level, and abilities. Be sure to increase the intensity or the cue until the horse responds.

Sometimes people will think that this means a horse whisperer will never get firm with a horse. This is untrue. It means that if a horse whisperer gets firm with a horse, it will be fair, focused on a goal, and is geared toward communicating an intention with the horse. Just like lead horses in the herd will bite or kick when required, although rarely, the horse whisperer may also reach those similar high intensity cues.

Another aspect to remember when increasing intensities in your cues is that horses generally think in 3-5 second intervals. This means that if a horse is not responding to a cue, you should increase the intensity of the cue within 3-5 seconds. Otherwise the horse may think the two events are unrelated and that you are just playing a desensitization game.

5) **Encounter, Wait, Revisit.** In a natural environment, the horse is never forced to go near something scary or new. The horse may choose to go near something 'scary' or new because of curiosity and confidence. If you were to put something potentially scary in a paddock—such as a tarp—at first the horse will likely avoid this potentially dangerous "predator." After awhile the horse may get curious and decide to investigate, then retreat to safety, and then investigate again.

The ability to retreat to safety builds confidence in the horse, so that all the fear previously felt towards the scary new object is now turned to curiosity. The horse will investigate the new object, and as a result will be more confident to approach other new things in the future. If you want to instill confidence in your horse, ALLOW him to stop when something is scary! Then when he's ready you can back up or do a small circle and he will cross the threshold and proceed safely past whatever is scary. If you just kick him forward he may turn to fight-or-flight instincts and go running and/or bucking past the scary object.

Note that this doesn't mean you should let your horse stop and turn from something scary. When your horse refuses a jump, refuses to go into a scary corner of the ring, or encounters anything nerve racking, allow the horse to stop, but keep him facing the scary thing. Once the horse shows a sign of tension being released, do a small circle or back up a couple steps, and go right back to the scary thing. Continue these steps until the horse is comfortable and can go past/over the scary thing. Making sure to do these steps will teach your horse the pattern and build confidence, so next time you encounter something scary the horse will not need to revisit it as many times. Eventually you will have a horse that can jump anything, or go past anything.

6) **Geared toward a goal.** Horses should always be able to find the comfort or release of pressure because there should always be a purpose or goal being worked toward.

This means there is a focus in mind—a focus held by the leader (that's you!). At play in the herd, a horse may kick another horse, but there is always an obvious answer to stop the kicking—in most cases the simple way for a horse to find comfort is to simply move away and he will be left alone. Unless there is a release, or a comfort zone, then the horse will be confused and not understand the purpose of the negative behaviour.

For example, if a horse refuses a jump and you smack him several times for it, he will not understand where the comfort is, and will instead become fearful at jumps and fearful of the rider. This may lead the horse to start racing towards/after jumps/bucking after fences/or will lose the will to work for the rider.

Another example is getting your horse to go in a trailer. The horse can be in the process of walking forward onto the trailer, but you are tapping him or harassing him anyway. How then is he supposed to know which direction to go when he is bothered for both going forward and standing still? Notice that if this is your method, then the horse is likely to stop even farther away next time from the trailer. In my experience I have worked with horses that refused to go closer than 50 feet to a trailer because of the negative memories associated with them.

7) **Act like a partner.** Most important in natural horsemanship is the recognition that the horse is biologically a prey animal, and the human is biologically a predator. You must turn this prey/predator relationship into a partnership. Humans like to control and manipulate, whereas horses' natural instincts are to avoid humans because of our predator characteristics—we walk in straight lines, we have eyes on the front of our heads, and we like to trap and control.

To get away from acting like a predator, put your focus on communication. When working with your horse think 'How can I best tell my horse what I want him to do?' 'Is this consistent?' 'Why did my horse react this way and what is he trying to tell me?' Try to understand your horse and recognize when he is asking for clarification, when he is confused or scared, rather than misinterpreting it as "misbehaving." Reviewing common communication signals can help you to read your horse.

Getting Started

Reading Horse Behaviour

Being able to read your horse and understand what he/she is saying is vital to your relationship. Communication works two ways in natural horsemanship. Your horse should listen and follow, while you must listen to your horse for feedback and be available for clarification.

Many people understand the basics of reading horse behaviour such as pinning ears is bad, and a relaxed posture is good, but few can recognize when a horse is asking a question or telling you he is frustrated. It is important to recognize and understand various ways your horse will communicate with you and other horses so that you understand when a horse is testing you, or when a horse is just lacking confidence.

Common Communication Signals (CCS) from Horses

Bucking

Bucking is an aggressive action and could be due to pain or asserting dominance or challenging leadership. Bucking is equivalent to kicking in that it is a potentially dangerous threat. Bucking can come in varying degrees—the horse may do a little buck as a warning. If nothing changes, then the horse may buck higher, or buck with a kick. Sometimes horses use a buck paired with a kick to give a more powerful kick, and also it allows them to kick with both back legs.

Crow Hopping

Think of crow hopping as when the horse jumps little invisible jumps, or as if they were hopping over crows. Horses crow hop when they are being playful and full of energy and occasionally because they are uncomfortable. Most of the time a horse will crow hop because he's excited and full of energy. You should note whether or not the ears are pinned. If the ears are pinned then the action is not playful. Sometimes horses will crow hop if they have not been worked in a while, or if the footing is bad in the paddock (too icy, too hard, too muddy, and/or too slippery), which leads to a fresh horse because he hasn't had a chance to run and play. When this happens you can teach your horse to control his energy and work on tasks to keep him focused such as circles, transitions, and bending. If the horse has good reason to be fresh, then you can get off and lunge or free lunge and allow him to have some play time before you hop back on and finish your ride.

Crowding you (standing really close to you, usually putting you at the horse's shoulder)

Crowding is something a horse does when he lacks confidence. The horse moves in very close to you and may even push on you enough to cause you to step aside. Protect your space by using your fingertips to keep the horse at a comfortable distance, but be careful not to get overly aggressive—use the minimum amount of force needed to protect your space. Have periods where you ask the horse to do something that pushes him out of the comfort zone, and then allow him in closer to you and work on things in the comfort zone, making sure that you never force a horse through a threshold, and never let him move your feet (protect your personal space).

Flicking Ears

Horses flick their ears to listen. They can turn an ear from the front to the side and back. Their ears can move independently of each other. When working with a horse, at least one of the ears should be flicking back toward you every few seconds to show that he's checking in with you. When the ears are constantly flicked toward you it means the horse is listening. If the horse's ears are constantly flicking in many directions from ahead to towards you, and all over, this could mean your horse is distracted or over stimulated. Just be aware that your horse is processing a lot of information, working on a difficult or new task, or is in a place where he feels less secure and is constantly scanning the area. It's a good sign if his ears are steady and focused on you. If the ears are never flicking towards you (not even once a minute) then he likely isn't paying much or any attention to you. You can get a horse to check in with you simply by asking for something, either a halt, back up, half halt to rebalance, circle, transition, etc. and you'll notice your horse check in with his ears.

Head Tossing

Head tossing is a sign of frustration, pain, high energy, or play. If the horse pins his ears or swishes his tail while head tossing then it means he's upset. It could be pain or he may be protesting a cue to go forward because you're asking for too much energy or work from him—at least he thinks you are. If he's tossing his head but not pinning his ears and not swishing his tail, then it's a sign of play. He may even jump on the spot (crow hopping). This can be due to an excess of energy, lack of exercise, or sometimes horses can get anxious and excited on windy or stormy days.

Horses can get more excited on windy or stormy days because it is harder to detect where predators are hiding due to the noise and movement of the wind, so the horses just get high on adrenaline, are on full alert, and are full of energy. As long as pain is ruled out and your cue is fair, you can press onward with whatever your cue was and do not release until you get the desired response. When you get what you asked for, release and reward by giving the horse a break. If you suspect the horse is fresh, you can lunge the horse or free lunge to allow him to play and get his energy out before you get back to work.

You also want to make sure that you are not the cause of frustration. Horses can get frustrated with their riders when they hit their back hard, make them feel unbalanced, are too rough with their hands, as well as many more reasons.

Horses may also head toss from trying to get away from flies or bugs, but this should be easy to recognize because if bugs are the reason then the horse should only be head tossing when bugs are near.

Many times head tossing will be related to a poor saddle fit—sometimes something as simple as just having the saddle too far forward, which blocks the shoulder movement. Horses that only head toss into the canter likely have an issue with the saddle fit.

High Head Set

If the horse's head is higher than when at liberty, then he's likely anxious about something unless you're purposely holding a horse's head up with short reins/a constricting device, or the horse could be avoiding contact with the bit (if you are using a bit). It could be that you're working in an unfamiliar or scary area, or if you are riding and the horse's head is up it could be that the saddle is uncomfortable or that he is anxious with you on his back because he doesn't fully trust and respect you on the ground. Check your saddle fit. To check if a horse is ready for you to ride just hop off and mount again—if you can mount with the horse standing still without anyone holding him then he's accepting of you. If he tries to walk off then you need to do some more ground work and mounting work to establish trust and respect.

Kicking

An aggressive threat and could be due to pain, asserting dominance, or challenging leadership. Watch for pinned ears or pursed lips as a warning sign.

Low Head Set

If the horse's head is being carried straight out from the withers, then this means he's relaxed. If the head is carried extremely low at liberty then he may be stretching his back, or showing a sign of submissiveness.

Pawing

Pawing is a sign of being bored and impatient. You can build patience in a horse by slowly increasing the amount of time your horse spends standing still or tied. When a horse paws, wait for him to stop pawing before you untie and move him elsewhere, otherwise you may condition him to paw because he'll think pawing gets your attention. Sometimes a horse will paw when eating his food—that's a natural response from times gone by when horses would have to paw to find food under snow, or in the ground (like carrots). Be watchful of these horses because they may eat too quickly and could choke.

Pursed Lips

Observe your horse relaxed when in a field or at liberty (no halter, tack, etc., just loose in the field/pen). The lips should be relaxed unless eating. When a horse purses his lips the muscles tighten and nostrils tense. The easiest way to note this is by noticing the nostril size. When the horse purses, the nostrils will have a slightly smaller opening and will be less round in shape.

Pursed lips can sometimes be the precursor to biting. Pursing lips is a subtle way to say 'I am not happy.' This could be due to pain, frustration, or general discontent from either being asked to do something they would rather not, or because they are challenging your leadership.

When a horse purses his lips, first ask yourself "What did I just do?" If you're tightening the girth it is likely that the horse is feeling uncomfortable—so be polite with the girth and tighten it slowly and in stages. Tighten the girth enough that the saddle will not fall, then move the horse forward, tighten again, move the horse forward again and tighten for a third time. You can tighten the girth again once you are mounted if you are able to (as with an English saddle).

If your horse purses his lips when you enter his stall or when you approach him, it's likely he does not accept your role as leader or because your relationship is not positive with your horse. If you have been too aggressive or demanding with the horse in the past, when he sees you he thinks negative thoughts and purses his lips. When a horse purses his lips, be aware that this could be a precursor to biting, so act appropriately.

Pinning Ears

Many people notice when a horse's ears are pinned, but sometimes when a horse turns his ears backward to listen behind, people mistake this for pinning ears.

Pinning ears is an expression of negative feeling either because of pain, anger, or discomfort of some kind. When a horse pins his ears, be aware that he may kick or bite if provoked. Discomfort could be from his personal space being threatened—for instance, when a horse passes too close to you while riding, hitting a rail when jumping, being asked to perform a difficult task, or many other similar situations.

When you notice the ears pinning, you need to recognize if you should back off or continue. If your horse is pinning his ears because you are asking him to move, which is establishing your dominance, continue to ask him to move. If he is pinning ears because he doesn't want you touching a certain part of his body, then wait for a positive expression while continuing to touch that particular spot, and then retreat to the comfortable spot. Then retry touching the 'bad' spot until he responds positively right away. You do not want to back away when a horse pins his ears because then you condition the horse to learn that pinning his ears will get you to back away. However, consider your own competence level and whether you have the savvy to work through the situation. You may need the help of your arm extension stick so you can stay further away from the horse at a safe distance, or the help of an experienced horse whisperer.

Dealing with the situation in this way you condition a horse to learn that if he gives you a positive/happy response and complies, then you will retreat and reward rather than push forward and demand more.

Remember that if the horse is pinning his ears as he canters, or every time you tighten the girth, or every time you jump, you should consider that your horse may be in pain and ensure proper tack fit and health.

Pricked Ears

If a horse has pricked ears and it lasts nearly a minute or more, and his body is tense, it generally means he's nervous or unsure about something. Horses can have their ears pointed towards something of interest and their bodies will remain relaxed. It is when a horse's body becomes tense in combination with pricked ears that you should suspect the horse is feeling some anxiety.

A horse's natural response to being startled is to freeze, look, and possibly snort. When humans punish horses for these actions by kicking them forward into work or yanking on them to stop snorting, then we teach our horses to go into fight-or-flight mode. This means the horse is more likely to buck, strike, and/or take off when scared. Being a prey animal, horses are primarily concerned with not being eaten/staying safe, so they will try to run from or fight whatever is hindering their safety.

If the horse's ears are pricked forward but the body is still relaxed (both in movement and in mind), then it just means his focus is on something else. He is focusing on something in whatever direction the ears are pricked. As a leader and handler just be aware of what the horse is focused on. You may need to get your horse to check in with you because he could be looking at a scary rock up ahead, or he may just be noticing cows in the next field.

In summary, pricked ears with a tense body is a watch out sign, and pricked ears with a relaxed body is nothing to be worried about—but be aware of what has your horse's attention as it could become scary if left unchecked. To work with a scared horse, see Dealing with the Scary Stuff for a detailed explanation and step-by-step guide.

Lowering Head with Pinned Ears

If a horse does this it is an aggressive threat and means 'watch out.' A horse will buck or kick when upset due to pain, frustration, or discomfort. Assess the situation to determine the problem. If you are riding and the horse is doing this to challenge your leadership, get off and re-establish your leadership and respect on the ground.

Quick and Jolty Steps

The horse is anxious either about the environment or about you and what you are teaching. Take things slowly and make sure trust and respect are established on the ground. If the horse is frightened of something then address the problem—see Dealing with the Scary Stuff for a detailed explanation and step-by-step guide.

Raising a Hind Leg

Threatening to kick is usually paired with pinned ears or a swishing tail and is an aggressive threat—be careful! Lifting a leg could also be a sign of pain in that leg. Note that raising a hind leg is different from resting a hind leg. Many horses will rest one of their back legs; the difference is that a horse who is threatening will actually have the hoof off the ground.

Rearing

A rearing horse is trying to get away from something that could be environmental, such as a dog running near by. They could also be trying to get away from the handler/rider, asserting dominance/challenging leadership or just simply trying to escape. Rearing is an action of trying to escape from something and if unsuccessful from a rear a horse may try taking off or striking. If you are ever on a horse when he rears, make sure you lean forward otherwise the horse could lose his balance and fall backwards onto you.

Smooth Steps

The horse is relaxed and comfortable.

Looking at You with Both Eyes

The horse is giving you his full attention and is not pressured by you. This is a good sign, full of respect and readiness.

Striking

Striking is when a horse uses a front leg to try to hit you. Striking refers to action from the front legs, whereas kicking refers to action from the hind legs.

This is an aggressive threat caused by the horse asserting dominance, challenging leadership, or trying to escape because they are scared. This horse may rear.

Swishing of the Tail

A horse swishing his tail is irritated. This could be due to pain, a difficult task, or an uncomfortable situation. Pain could be from ill-fitting tack or a sore leg. Difficult tasks could include anything new or advanced like flying lead changes. Uncomfortable situations could be feeling crowded—for example when another horse rides too close.

A swishing tail paired with pinned ears signifies the horse is likely about to kick or buck. If the swishing tail is due to pain it's unlikely the horse will kick, unless you're provoking the situation either by tightening the girth or moving the horse into a faster gait like a canter or asking him to jump—the pain may cause him to buck or kick out.

Turning the Head Away From You

If you are working on the ground and your horse's body is facing you but he turns his head from you, it's because he feels pressured by you. You as a predator have a lot of pressure coming from your body. Try turning your belly button away from the horse, or just turning yourself sideways. Your horse will likely swing his head back around and face you with both eyes. As your relationship builds, the horse will get more comfortable and you will have to turn your body less to the side and soon the horse will be comfortable when you're facing him.

Turning the Whole Body from You

This is a sign of disrespect or unwillingness to engage at the moment. If the horse is turning his hindquarters towards you, then you should shoo him away by putting pressure on him with your rope, or whatever is necessary to move him away. He may kick, so stay out of the kick zone (10 feet behind the horse). You want to move him away to assert your leadership for two reasons 1) protect your space and 2) by moving the horse forward the horse is still following your lead.

There are different vocal and non-vocal sounds that a horse can make. These include: the nicker and whinny (very similar), the squeal, the roar/blowing, the sigh/ soft snort, and the sneeze.

Blowing/Roar

Blowing/roaring is typically done when a horse is startled or unsure. It is a harsh loud noise, very abrupt and distinct. When a horse blows he may be in flight-or-fight mode, and you may also notice him raising his tail as a warning sign to other horses to stay clear. You can often see a horse do this if you chase him when at liberty. Note that some horses may have a condition called a 'roar', which causes them to make a sound when being exercised that sounds like a roar. This is caused by a nerve improperly functioning and can surgically be corrected in most cases, although the condition usually does not affect the horse for working/riding unless excessive demands are made on the horse such as racing or high endurance, because the oxygen demand cannot be met.

Neigh or Whinny

High pitched and drawn out sound that carries over a fair distance. A horse will whinny to call when other horses may be in sight or not. When taking a horse off property for the first time, a horse may call more often if he came with a buddy of his. This is because once separated at the show he knows his buddy should be within whinny ear shot although he may not see him.

When a horse whinnies there is no need to be scared, but just keep in mind the horse is distracted and may be feeling a little uneasy, which is why he is calling to his buddies. Try and give the horse a focus by asking him to do something that gets him thinking, like moving sideways, doing a haunch turn or backing up. You do not want to just lunge him in circles because although you may physically tire the horse, you are doing nothing mentally engaging. Be aware that if you are handling a horse on the ground who is whinnying, he may push into you to move around to search for the other horse so be very aware of your space, and work with the horse at a distance if possible (hold near the end of the rope or reins if possible) and control the horse using "pushing the air" techniques—this will keep you safer than if you are right up close to the horse.

Nickering

The softest of the horse's vocal categories, this is a pleasant noise and should not cause any alarm. Some horses may nicker as you bring them treats or come to get them. It is a soft call of excitement, attention getting, and positive thoughts. Mothers and foals nicker to each other and your horse's friends may nicker when leaving or returning to a paddock.

Sighing/Soft Snorting

Sounds like a deep exhale from breathing out. Sighing can mean the horse is relaxed and generally means he's in a calmer state of mind, or the horse could just be expulsing something from the respiratory tract—either way it's nothing to be alarmed about.

Sneeze

A sneeze is a forceful exhale to rid anything foreign in the nose. When riding on a dusty trail or dusty ring the horse may sneeze more—if your horses sneezes frequently, even in dusty environments, your horse may have allergies and you should consult a veterinarian.

Squeal

A squeal is a high-pitched noise, often quite loud, that a horse usually makes when challenging or meeting new horses. In the wild, stallions will squeal and have a dominance fight. The outcome of the fight will be indicated based on the stallion who defecates last, or if it is a tie then they will walk away from each other and defecate at the same time. If a horse squeals at you, you should be careful because the horse may challenge you.

In Summary

When looking at a horse, remember the following meanings:

If the horse's ears are:

- Neutral: The ears are held loosely upward, openings facing forward or outward. This means the horse is calm, thinking, listening, relaxed, or tired.

- Pricked: Ears held stiff with openings pointed directly forward means the horse is alert and focused on something.

- Airplane ears: The ears flop out laterally with openings facing down; usually meaning the horse is tired, in deep thought, agitated, in pain, or depressed.

- Angled backward (with openings directed back towards a rider): Usually mean attentiveness to the rider or listening to commands.

- Pinned flat against the neck: This means watch out! The horse is angry and potentially aggressive.

If the head is:

- High: Alert and potentially nervous (well above the withers).

- Medium to Low: Calm (at or slightly above the withers).

- Really Low: Sign of submission, unless the head is low with pinned ears which means a threat and they may potentially bite (below the withers).

If the tail is:

- High: Alert or excited (horses' tails can actually stand straight up like a deer's tail).

- Appears tucked or very low: It is a sign of exhaustion, fear, pain or submission.

- Swishing: Irritated (either at the handler, other horses/animals, or pestering bugs).

If a horse's legs are:

- Pawing: Bored/frustrated.

- One front leg lifted: Can be a mild threat or a sign of impatience (some horses do this when eating).

- A back leg lifted: Is often a more defensive threat.

- A back leg resting: Is just resting.

- Stamping: Probably just getting bugs off.

If the horse sounds:

- Loud or high pitched: Could be anxious or on high alert.

- Quiet or soft noises: Happy or relaxed.

These ears mean 'I'm alert and/or looking at something'

Lacking a little bit of confidence

Lacking a lot of confidence

These ears mean 'I'm listening'

These ears mean 'I'm angry'

These ears mean 'I'm listening to something behind me'

If the horse does:

- The Flehmen response (the horse sticks his nose in the air and curls his upper lip over his nose): He has experienced an interesting smell.

- Flaring nostrils: Usually means he is excited, alert, or really out of breath.

- Showing more white around the eyes than usual: Usually means he is angry or scared.

- Piercing lips: Mild sign of aggression—may progress if provoked.

REMEMBER: What a horse is saying is a combination of the whole body communicating, so what a horse is saying by tossing his/her head depends on what the other parts of the body are also communicating at the same time. Remember to look at the whole horse to determine what your horse is trying to tell you.

Learn About Your Horse

Start by observing your horse with his/her field mates. Watch how your horse plays and what rank your horse holds within the herd.

If your horse is the herd boss then you may face more resistance when asserting yourself as the leader. If your horse is very needy in the paddock, always with a buddy and/or tends to have bites from other horses because he gets pushed around, then you may have a horse that loves to crowd your space because he lacks confidence on his own. If your horse loves playing halter tag, or picks things up like jolly balls, sticks, or chews on other horses, then expect your horse to be very oral, meaning very active with his mouth. With this type of horse you'll have to be very aware of your personal space so you don't get bitten or get everything chewed. A horse who keeps to himself may work well on his own, whereas a horse that is always near his friends may get upset if you try and work away from other horses.

You can save yourself a lot of hassle with a clingy horse by leaving him in a small paddock by himself for a few days so he can develop independence and confidence on his own. Then you can reintroduce the horse back to his field mates and continue to occasionally (once a month or so) provide a few hours of individual turnout so your horse remembers he can be comfortable on his own.

It is best the first few times to do individual turnout in a place that still allows the horse to see his buddies, or even touch noses over the fence. The objective is to teach the horse to have independence from his herd mates. However, you do not want to overstress the horse.

Horses need to socialize and are best out in herds, but this is a great way to help your horse find some independence without putting any pressure on you to do anything other than to monitor him. Note that individual turnout exclusively is not recommended because then your horse cannot fulfill their social needs. This will put a lot of extra stress on the handler because the horse will be trying to fulfill his social needs with the handler such as play, determining rank, and grooming activities. Horses can become depressed and/or grumpy when deprived of companionship for long periods of time.

If your horse is the type to get upset, be careful not to do this on an extremely hot day where he may get heat stroke from running back and forth if he's pacing the fence trying to get back to his buddies. Be careful with young and out-of-shape horses that they do not strain joints or their health from pacing if they are quite upset and anxious. Generally a horse may run around for 10 to 15 minutes and then settle down with occasional bursts of trotting or calling. Be careful to only take the horse out of the round pen once he is calm—removing an anxious horse from the pen will only teach the horse to run around more next time. This is because the reward is in the release; the horse will think that the correct response was to call to his buddies and run around anxious because after those actions are when you returned him to his buddies.

Once you can lead your horse calmly into an area without other horses around, or turn him out without other horses, then you know your horse is not dependent on his herd mates. Introducing your horse to a new area, or an area by himself will normally take a few minutes for the horse to become calm and collected, but if it takes more than 15 minutes for him to settle when being handled, it may be a good idea to turn him alone for a few hours a day.

Having a strong relationship with your horse or having experience and being a competent horse whisperer will mean your horse will be less likely to feel dependent on his herd mates. This means that a horse may feel comfortable with a handler or with his herd mates, but may not be confident on his own. This is because when on his own he is without the protection of a leader to keep him safe.

Getting Organized

You should have a rope halter and an arm extension stick (which some horse whisperers call a carrot stick, handy stick, etc.) with a 5 to 6-foot piece of thin rope on the end.

The stick is simply an extension of your arm, allowing you to communicate at further distances, to ask a variety of skills and to give you confidence by giving you more space between you and the horse. The stick should be quite firm so that you can use it to press against the horse to ask him to move away (similar to using your own hand to ask a horse to move over). A lunge whip is not suitable because it is too flexible. You also want something fairly lightweight so your arm doesn't get tired.

You can make your own arm extension stick from a golf club, or a lightweight stick with a grip. Use tape to make a loop at the end to attach a 5 to 6-foot piece of rope. You want to be able to use your arm extension stick for close distances and longer distances when working with your horse. This is why you want to have a removable 5 to 6-foot rope attachment. This rope piece gives you more reach for when working with air pressure techniques (you will learn more about direct and air pressure further into the book). Having a detachable rope piece means that when you are working exclusively with direct pressure (close distances) you do not have to worry about getting tangled up with the rope and then the stick can be used when riding without fear of the horse stepping on the rope piece.

Extension sticks are available at many tack shops, or if you can't find one there, they're available online through various horse whisperer websites or even online auction websites. An increasing number of tack shops are starting to carry natural horsemanship tools either in stock or available through ordering. If you don't see it in stores, ask about ordering.

The halter should be made of thin and dense rope, and may have 2 or 4 knots across the noseband.

Rope halters provide better communication because the knots sit along facial nerves and provide clearer signals to the horse. This allows the horse to better feel the pressure and from which direction the pressure is coming. This aids in teaching horse signals and cues and helps to better develop your language with the horse.

Nylon or leather halters are designed to distribute pressure evenly. These halters are great for tying horses in, or horses that are left unsupervised because there is less chance of damage to the facial nerves.

Using a leather halter for tying the untrained or unsupervised horse is recommended because the leather can break if the horse panics and it is unlikely for there to be nerve damage from the halter. Rope halters are recommended for when working with horses and can be used for tying the trained horse (a horse that has been trained to give to pressure).

You should have a fairly thick 10 to 15-foot rope, heavy enough to allow for some feel, like yacht rope. The lead rope should have a heavy snap on the end that connects to the halter.

You want a long rope of 10 to 15 feet so that you can work with your horse from a safe distance if needed, so you can practice a variety of skills, to show better leadership by being able to manage a larger amount of space, and yet not too long as to get tangled up in the rope. As you become more advanced and organized in your technique, you will be able to advance to longer rope lengths.

Dense ropes have more feel that allow better manipulation from longer distances. You can test this out at tack stores by wiggling, swirling, and flinging different ropes. You want something that is soft enough to allow a wiggle, but not so soft or light that a wiggle gets lost midway down the rope. This will assist you when teaching your horse cues. The heavy snap at the end of the rope will allow you to 'bite the horse' in the chin if you need to go to an extreme intensity (just like horses may have to bite or kick their herd mates). You want the option to be able to bite.

Also the heavy snap provides steady feel of the halter on the horse. This means that when you lift the rope and therefore lift the snap, the horse feels the lift in pressure and gives you one more communication signal.

Practice with Your Tools Before You Start with Your Horse

Natural horsemanship is all about leadership and communication. If you show up to the paddock fumbling to do up the halter and then get tangled in your lead rope and trip over your stick, you're not going to appear like a confident leader to your horse. You also may confuse your horse. Take a few minutes to practice with your tools until you're comfortable before you go get your horse.

Things to practice:

- Be able to tie the rope halter knot.

- Be comfortable holding the long rope and able to lengthen, shorten, and move with the rope at different lengths while being careful never to wrap the rope around your hand. Either fold the rope and hold it, or just allow the rope to drag on the ground. You don't want to wrap the rope around your hand in case your horse takes off—you could get caught in the rope and dragged.

- Be able to use your stick with accuracy. Practice resting your stick at your side, then pick it up and touch a particular object or spot on a tree, wall, bench, etc. Be able to press against a wall with controlled and varying degrees of pressure. Be able to fling your string on the end of your stick at a particular spot on the wall or fence. Make sure you're accurate at different intensities and distances from objects.

- Clip your rope to a halter and hang the halter on a hook. Drop the rope and be able to pick up the rope using your foot or extension stick (by lifting the rope to your hands, NOT bending over). Bending over may confuse your horse.

- Practice flinging your lead rope out at a particular spot on a wall or fence (fling the end that does not have the clip).

- Walk around for a couple of minutes with your stick and rope in hand. Be aware of how much you move your body and your tools. If you are constantly readjusting your tools or flicking your stick you could be sending mixed signals to your horse, so practice moving around and simulate asking for different things while being aware of excessive movement. It helps to have a friend to practice with. Take turns being the horse and pretend to ask for different cues. Your friend can tell you how much pressure she feels, where she feels the pressure, and what she thinks you are trying to do. Be sure not to tell each other what type of horse you are going to be, and what your focus/cues are.

Page 65

Fitting and Tying the Rope Halter

The halter should fit with the knots sitting on the facial nerves. You can best assure this by making sure the noseband is not too high or too low on the horse and that the cheek pieces do not come too close to the eyes, but still sit midway on each side of the horse's face. The loop under the chin should not be too big so that the snap of the lead rope can make contact with the chin if you were to shake the lead rope firmly.

Steps to tying the rope halter:

1. Standing on the left side of your horse, place the horse's nose in the halter, and the crown/ free piece of rope over the horse's head and behind the ears.

2. Put the crown/free piece of rope that is over the horse's head and behind the horse's ears through the hole that is on the left side.

3. Then create a D like shape.

4. Put the free rope end through the D shape so that the end of the rope is flapping away from the horse's eye.

5. Pull the knot tight.

Tips for making it easy:

- Have the lead rope attached to the halter. This will help show you which way is down/up.

- Look for the section of the rope halter that is double roped. There will be two sections of the rope halter that have two parallel pieces of rope. The first sits under the chin and has the lead rope attachment at one end. The second sits across the horse's nose and has knots at either end of the section. Being able to identify these sections of the halter will help you with easily placing it on your horse.

- Start by reaching your right arm over the horse's neck, and use your left hand to pass the crown/free piece of rope to your right hand—this way you aren't trying to fling the rope over the horse. Then you can proceed with putting your horse's nose in the halter.

Tying a Rope Halter

1. Place the halter on the horse

2. Slip the free end through loop

3. Make a D shape

4. Place the free end through the D loop you just made

5. Pull tight

6. You're done!

Time to Meet Up With Your Horse

One of the first things you can do with your horse is just spend time in his paddock or stall doing absolutely nothing. Our horses are so used to us entering their space and commanding them to do things and then leaving them when we have gotten what we want.

You can do wonders for your relationship if you just take 10 to 30 minutes and spend time in his field or stall doing nothing. You can sit and observe your horse, or sit and read a book—perhaps this book! Try not to engage your horse at all—only touch your horse if he touches you first. Be careful to protect your space if you feel threatened, but otherwise leave the horse alone. It is best to do this in a small paddock, and preferably when it is just your own horse.

Doing this exercise will get the horse interested in you, and change negative perceptions that your horse may previously have had of you because you will be spending non-demanding time with him.

When you do meet up with your horse to start work, remember when leading him to give slack in the rope and allow the horse to follow you. Holding a horse right under the chin can make him feel trapped and anxious.

Also remember that to be a good leader, you must protect your herd. To start with, you will be a herd of two. You are one member of your herd, and your horse is another member of your herd. Once you are more experienced, you may start working with multiple horses at a time.

It is the leader's responsibility to protect the followers of the herd. That means your horse should be safe when he's with you. Be careful when taking a horse out of the herd that he doesn't get bitten or kicked by another horse when leaving. When in the barn aisle, or area tacking up, make sure no other horse harms your horse. It is your job to keep your horse safe. If another horse is able to bite or kick your horse while you are handling him, it will set your relationship back because your horse will be thinking, 'This leader cannot even protect me from other horses, I would be in real danger if a wolf were to come along.'

Teaching the Basics

Step 1: Teach That Your Tools are Friendly

You should be able to rub your tools all over your horse and fling them around the horse without him becoming upset.

Steps to teaching that your tools are friendly:

1. Start by offering a tool for him to sniff such as the halter, the rope, or your stick.

2. If the horse shies away, wait a moment until the horse is still, then take the tool away to a comfortable distance.

Teaching That Your Tools are Friendly

1. Cooper gets quite upset with the tools near him

2. At first Cooper is running from the tools

3. With patience Lindsey is able to get Cooper to accept the tools

4. Now with Cooper accepting of the tools, Lindsey can use them

3.   Offer the object again and repeat these steps until you can rub the horse all over.

Another trick is to drag the object—like the stick and string—behind you and start walking, asking your horse to follow at a distance he feels comfortable. Any fear will then turn to curiosity and the horse will get closer and closer to inspect the tool when he's ready.

When trying to rub the tool over certain areas on the horse, you may get resistance from the horse if he doesn't want you touching that area. Common sensitive areas on horses are the eyes, mouth, ears, belly, tail, and the buttocks/groin. If your horse gets tense when approaching any area, stay in that same spot and rub until he's a bit more relaxed or accepting. Wait for him to signal that he is more accepting—for some horses this might be lowering his head, relaxing his posture, or resting a foot. For others you might just be happy that he's stopped pinning his ears or has stopped threatening to kick. Once he relaxes and becomes accepting of the tool, then retreat from that sensitive area, and rub on an area where you know he's comfortable.

Usually horses are comfortable with people rubbing their necks and shoulders and it is a good place to start. Do this same routine if the horse walks off—keep rubbing in the same spot, while using a free hand to help stop the horse if needed, and only stop rubbing once the horse is accepting of the tool. The idea is that the horse will understand that nothing is being asked, that these tools will not hurt him and that if he is accepting you will retreat and reward by moving to an area he enjoys. The other important concept you are teaching him is that if he does become more accepting, you will not abuse that trust by pursuing further; instead you will retreat and start over.

When playing with your horse with this introductory step, try to find the 'sweet spots' that he loves having rubbed—common sweet spots on horses can be found near the withers, the chest, and the underside of the head/neck.

Problems with horses behaving poorly for the vet, farrier, for saddling, or bathing and clipping typically need work with this step. This is the only desensitizing step. All the other steps are sensitizing activities meaning you want a response from touching your horse. During this step you are simply asking the horse to stay still.

Start with soft rubs and spots on your horse that you think your horse will like, then advance to sensitive areas and more dramatic movements, or 'scarier' tools.

Step 2: Develop Basic Cues

In order to develop a language with your horse, you need to start with basic cues and movements. These can later be built upon to include more advanced movements and lead to more skills in the future. The basic movements your horse can perform are forwards, backwards, move the front end (haunch turn), move the back end (forehand turn), move sideways, and go over. More advanced skills include go up (rear) and go down (lying down). All of these can be taught to your horse.

Because going up and down are more advanced skills, they are best left to being taught after the other movements are well understood.

A couple things to know:

There are two ways you can ask a horse to do something: either by touching him or not touching him. The first is called direct pressure and the second is called air pressure. Direct pressure is when you are directly touching the horse and air pressure is when you are touching the air. You should be able to ask your horse for all of the basic movements with both direct pressure and air pressure.

Remember that the horse thinks in short intervals of about 3 to 5 seconds, so if you are asking for a cue and meet resistance, or the horse does not respond, you need to increase the intensity of that cue quickly, otherwise the horse may not make an association. For example, if you are asking a horse to back up by wiggling your rope, and you wiggle the rope politely for a minute or so before moving the rope more quickly, and then wait another minute before moving the rope a little more quickly, he may not realize that each stage had anything to do with the other. He may just think you're trying to teach him to be tolerant of a jiggling rope.

As long as your horse is trying to figure out what you want, do not increase intensity. This means that if the horse is giving any sign of trying to figure out what you are doing, do not change the cue. This is because when the horse responds in any way, you are giving enough pressure to get a response—you just have to wait for the correct response. Increasing intensity could make the horse nervous, agitated, or flighty. The only exception is if the horse is moving into your space, then you may need to be more assertive in order to protect your space. For example, if you are asking the horse to back up by pressing into the horse's chest, and he just starts bobbing his head—you have stimulated a response, just not the right one, so **keep the same pressure** until the horse actually starts backing up. Then immediately **reward by releasing** the pressure.

When first starting with your horse, you may be using long phases of 20 to 45 seconds with each level of intensity. As your horse starts to understand your cues, you should be quicker and increase the intensity of your cues within 15 seconds if your horse is not responding. When more advanced you should be increasing intensities of your cues within 10 seconds or less if there is no response from your horse. It's a good idea to give a more generous time-frame to the ideal cue (about 15 seconds) but then move more quickly through increasing intensity cues until you get the desired response. This really makes it easy for the horse to figure out what is desired and what is not, because the comfort of the ideal cue is so easy to realize, and the discomfort of not responding intensifies fairly quickly so the horse is motivated to respond from the ideal cue and not just 'wait it out' to see if you give up.

Recognize when your horse is digesting a thought. Horses will usually show signs of digesting a thought by chewing or licking their lips, as long as they didn't just eat, or by lowering the head level below the withers and letting out a sigh. Wait for these signs, and allow the horse to finish digesting the thought before advancing. Trying to progress too quickly will not allow the horse enough time to process thoughts and may get your horse frazzled.

Recognize when your horse is asking a question. Every time a horse flicks an ear toward you, or when he turns and faces you, he's asking you a question. Be patient and polite, and start over from the ideal cue again—do not add any more pressure—just be patient because he is trying! *Never ask for more when the horse is already trying* and *never punish a horse for asking a question*. Also be careful to quickly answer the horse's question, otherwise he may think the correct response was to face you and ask you a question (rather than performing whatever task you were trying to ask for).

Understanding Pressure

When working with your horse, understand that where you send or put pressure on a horse is the area that you want to move. Horses should move away from pressure. More specifically, a horse should only move the body area affected by the pressure.

This means if you put pressure in front of a horse he should move backward. If you put pressure between the side of the head and the shoulder he should just move the front end. Pressure at the barrel should mean sideways. Pressure at the side of the hind end should just move the hind, and pressure behind the horse should send him forward. If you move backwards, it should draw a horse towards you. You can also send a horse in the direction you want by pointing in the direction you want him to go, and then following up with pressure elsewhere on the horse to get what you want (go to the 'round abouts' section to learn more about sending a horse in a direction).

Your belly button and eyes house a great deal of pressure. This means that when you face a horse right on, both your belly button and eyes staring the horse down, you are pointing a lot of pressure at the horse. If you pair this with actually walking toward the horse, the horse may move away depending on how confident a horse he is. If the horse has medium confidence, he may not move away, but may raise his head and look off to the side, as if to say, 'Whoa, why so much pressure?'

Try to *remember that your belly button is a third eye*, and you should always be looking in the direction you want the horse to go. Also when inviting a horse into your space, you should turn off one of your eyes by turning your belly button off to the side creating less pressure on the horse and thus telling him it is okay to enter your space. Lastly when you walk towards a horse and he starts to move away (but you don't want him to), think about how you can turn your belly button pressure off. We predators like to walk in straight lines. Try walking in swerved patterns so that you aren't directing so much pressure at the horse. Think like a horse—an animal coming straight at you is usually a danger, whereas an animal that swerves a bit in his path is not coming straight at you and poses less danger.

This logic about straight lines versus swerved patterns holds true for many prey animals. I think back to memories on my friend's farm that had chickens. One day we were catching the chickens to move them back into their hutches. If we walked directly toward a chicken we had no hope of catching it. However, we could get right next to one if we did a weaving, unpredictable, swerved pattern, and then once beside the chicken we could pick it up easily. Many prey animals are like this.

Another example to demonstrate this phenomenon is when you see deer out on a trail ride. You will notice that when you come across deer on a trail ride, that if you stop and stare at them, they are likely to run away. You have a better chance of the deer staying in place for a picture if you keep walking in a weaving pattern past them. Just remember to keep your eyes and belly buttons facing away from them.

Pressure can be created from many movements—a swirl of your stick or rope, the flapping of your arm, or even just by crouching a little and making a stern face at your horse. Understanding where you are directing your pressure is of utmost importance. Practicing the different cues with another human pretending to be a horse (no talking!) will let you get comfortable with your tools and practice directing pressure—with the added benefit of verbal feedback when you're done.

When working with your horse, be specific with your cues and where you are directing pressure. For example, if your horse starts to back up when you are trying to go sideways, first establish what pressure area you are activating—ask yourself: Is your rope too tight? Are you pulling your horse backward without noticing? Is the pressure too far forward?

Also when teaching the pressure areas it is very important to only stop asking when you get what you want otherwise you will teach the wrong pressure area to move the wrong way. So when asking for sideways and the horse backs up, keep asking for sideways until the horse goes sideways. This follows the principle 'the reward is in the release.' Just be sure you are putting pressure in the right area.

One of the ways to understand where your pressure areas are is to have a horse free (no halter or rope attached) in the round pen and ask him to go forward, stop and change direction. You will learn how much notice the horse needs, and how much pressure to use. If you are too aggressive or passive in your movements, the horse will speed up or ignore you.

Teaching the Basic Cues through Direct Pressure

For many this may seem very basic, and may even be common practice for some movements. It is important to establish that you can ask for all the basic movements, that you are understood, and that your horse moves fairly freely without great resistance.

Understanding Pressure: Playing Join Up

Above: Following the horse causes the horse to want to look at you

Above & Below Left: Lindsey backs up when the horse looks at her, which draws the horse in towards her; instead of Lindsey walking at the horse's head to capture the horse, which may send the horse away

Above Right: The horse has chosen to come to Lindsey, so the horse stands quietly as Lindsey prepares the halter

Following the Feel in the Rope
1. Reach the rope over 2. & 3. Slide the rope behind the horse
4. & 5. Gently pull the rope towards you 6. You're done!

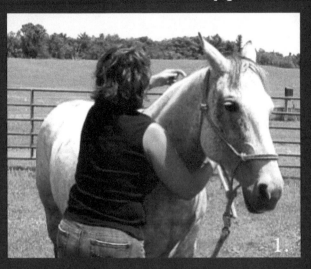

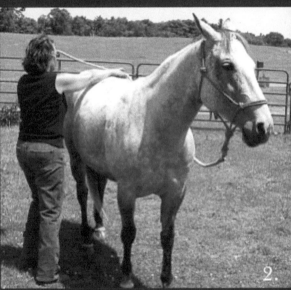

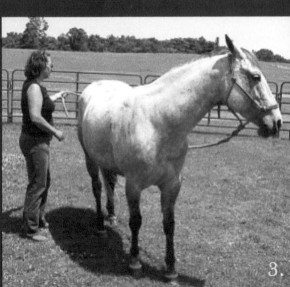

Backing Up with Direct Pressure

1. to 4. Ashley uses direct pressure on Canterbury's chest to ask her to back up.

You can also apply direct pressure using your stick and pressing the chest, or by using your hand and pressing on the horse's nose (be careful not to block the horse's breathing!)

Always remember to start with your ideal cue, whatever cue you would ideally like your horse to move from. You must always start with the ideal cue and increase the intensity as needed to get the result.

Moving Forward

There are two main ways to ask a horse to go forward: 1) either by drawing the horse into you, by backing away from the horse, or using a cue directed at the front end that signals 'come' such as patting your leg, and 2) using pressure behind the horse to drive the horse forward.

Steps to asking a horse to move forward:

1. You can ask your horse to move forward towards you by standing at the end of your rope and applying light pressure on the halter.

2. If the horse does not move forward, slowly add more pressure to the rope so that there is greater pressure on the halter. If your horse walks forward, immediately release the tension on the rope—remember the reward is in the release. If he resists, keep pressure on the halter, and continue to add pressure as needed.

3. If your horse is resisting and you feel you are pulling quite hard on the rope, keep the tension on the rope but ask on an angle which may require your horse to shift his balance and take a step forward (pulling the rope off to the left or right, not straight ahead).

Once your horse understands, try standing at different positions and having him come towards you. Eventually you may be able to stand beside the hind end and direct your horse in a semi-circle towards you because he'll learn to follow the feel in the rope.

To learn how to send a horse forward, refer to the 'round abouts' section.

Moving Backward

Steps to back up your horse using direct pressure:

1. Stand in front of your horse, facing him. Use your stick to press gently on his chest (your belly button faces the direction you want the horse to go).

2. When your horse steps backward, release the pressure. If he resists, add more pressure and be patient until he steps backward. Be sure to release pressure as soon as he complies. Release pressure by going back to a friendly rub—you don't want to teach your horse to try and avoid pressure entirely. This is because once riding your leg will still stay resting at the horse's side.

Forehand Turn (moving the haunches) through Direct Pressure

1. Andrea begins with her ideal cue to ask Elsie to move her haunches. You can see Elsie asking Andrea a question by flicking her ear back toward Andrea.

2. Elsie begins the forehand turn and Andrea walks in the direction of travel so that she can keep her hand on Elsie to maintain direct pressure.

3. We can see Elsie doing the turn perfectly because her left hind leg is crossing over her right hind leg. This is also how we disengage the horse (by getting the horse to cross over its hind legs).

4. Here we can see Elsie move her left front leg just a little bit, so Andrea corrects her by bumping the rope to stop the movement going forward.

5. Andrea and Elsie completing the forehand turn.

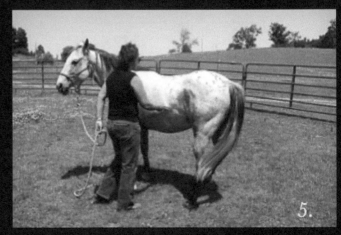

If you are sure your horse will not nip and if you are comfortable, you can use your hand on his chest and press with your finger tips. You can also press the horse's nose to ask him to back up, but this can be more difficult because the horse may just try and move its head away from the pressure.

Forehand Turn (move the haunches)

Steps to complete a forehand turn through direct pressure:

1. Stand beside the haunches of your horse, or just in front of the haunches, facing your horse. Hold your rope in the hand closest to your horse's head (it will change depending on what side you are on).

2. Press on the side of the horse near the haunches. Ideally you want to press in the same spot or near the same spot that you can press when in the saddle. Start with your ideal pressure, then increase after about ten seconds and increase again and again until you get the desired response. Release when you get the desired result. Release pressure by returning to the friendly rubbing; you don't want to teach your horse to try and avoid pressure entirely. This is because once riding your leg will still stay resting at the horse's side.

Once the horse understands the concept, you can ask for several steps by asking, then softening the cue (go back to the ideal cue) as the horse moves (but not completely releasing pressure) and then pressing again to ask for more steps, being sure to soften after every step.

If the horse walks forward you can use your rope to stop him, or if he's completely confused you can pull his head towards you with one hand, and keep pressing with the other hand on his side, this will better clarify things for the horse. Then release when he moves the hind legs.

Unless you are stopping the horse from moving forward you should not put pressure on his head at all for at least a minute to give him a chance to figure out what you are doing. Add pressure to the rope (pulling the horse's head toward you) only if your horse is still confused. This will cause his hind legs to move away from you - your desired goal. Ideally you want the horse to pivot on the front foot.

Trouble Shooting:

This is usually the easiest of the basic cues, but sometimes a horse will go forward, or try to just walk away (thinking you are giving a cue to leave). Be sure to have the lead rope in hand so that you can direct the horse's nose toward you by pulling on the rope if he gets confused, and also so that you can bump the rope to stop him from going forward. Be quick to correct as soon as he takes one foot forward because you want to be very clear about what you are asking.

The horse may not be paying attention when you give the ideal cue. *It is the horse's responsibility to pay attention to you*. You ask, and if the horse misses the ideal cue from

Haunch Turn (moving the front end) through Direct Pressure

1. Andrea begins with her ideal cue; her right hand presses on Elsie. Andrea is ready to use her left hand to help direct Elsie away from her if Elsie does not understand her ideal cue.

2. From this angle you can better see the placement of Andrea's hand which is asking the front end to move away from her. She is placing her hand in a spot that her leg could reach when riding her.

3. What a lovely haunch turn! You can see Elsie doing a nice cross over with her front legs; this allows Elsie's right hind leg to stay in the same spot.

4. In this photo you can see Andrea using her left hand to support her ideal cue. Andrea's left hand is helping to guide Elsie away from her.

5. Another nice cross over in front shows that Elsie is doing the turn correctly.

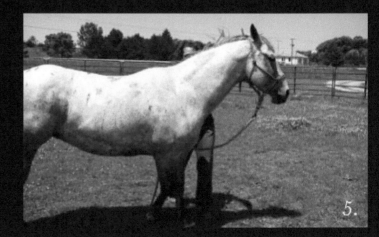

lack of attention, then progress to the higher intensity cue. The horse will start to learn to watch you more carefully and be more attentive in order to look for the ideal cues, to avoid the higher intensity cues. Therefore do not wait for the horse's attention before you start asking; just start with your ideal cue, and increase intensity.

Haunch Turn (move the front end)

Steps to completing a haunch turn using direct pressure:

1. Stand beside your horse facing him at the shoulder or just in front of the shoulder. Put the rope in the hand that is furthest from the horse's head (this will change depending on what side you are standing). The free hand should be placed on the side of the horse near the front but not beyond his nose. This hand acts as a guide and blocks the horse from walking into you. It may also direct the head away from you if the horse doesn't understand the cue from the other hand. Place your hand holding the rope behind the shoulder, or on the shoulder. Ideally you want to place your free hand somewhere you could also press when riding.

2. Start with your ideal cue and press the hand holding the rope into the horse, asking him to move. Increase the pressure until the horse moves his front end away from you. Release pressure as soon as the horse moves from you.

If the horse walks forward, bump the rope until he stops going forward, but keep asking the horse to move the front end until he moves it away from you. Ideally you want the horse to pivot on a back foot. You can also do this exercise by standing beside the horse's head and pressing on the side of the head and neck to move the front end, which is helpful for ground manners, but not ideal for when trying to teach the horse a cue that can also be done in the saddle.

Horses tend to walk forward when doing this at first—be very quick to correct when this happens. Make sure your body is facing the direction you want to go. If the horse moves his head down, then just walk into him and bump the horse with your foot (lightly—you only want to show the horse it is uncomfortable to have the head that low, and you do not want to hurt the horse—especially the eye).

Trouble Shooting:

Sometimes this can be a tricky move because the horse raises his head and tries to move it to the other side, or because he walks forward. If the horse is raising his head, then stand at the shoulder and put more pressure on it, using your free hand (the one not holding the rope) to block the horse's head from going over you, and guide him in the direction you want to go. You may want to use your extension stick to block the horse's head from going over you if this is a problem.

If the horse is walking forward, stand slightly in front of the shoulder and literally walk into the horse in the direction you want him to go. That way your body is being very clear about the direction you want to go (while still using your hands for pressure), and be very quick to 'bump' the rope to stop the horse if he walks forward. Have the rope length fairly short so it is easy for you to bump the rope.

Move Sideways

Steps to teaching your horse to move sideways through direct pressure:

1. Stand slightly behind the horse's shoulder at his side, facing him. Have the rope in your hand closest to his head.

2. Your free hand should place pressure on the side of the horse, in the middle of the two spots that you use for a forehand and haunch turn.

3. Apply your ideal amount of pressure on the horse's side and release when he moves sideways. Be sure to keep your horse from walking forward by bumping the rope if needed. Move one step at a time and be patient!

This should be taught last of all the direct pressure moves because it is more complex and requires the horse to move both the front end and the back end together.

Trouble Shooting:

If your horse is confused, try moving the front end, then the back end, then try both ends together. If you get stuck again just start with the front end and then ask the back end to catch up until your horse understands. As soon as the horse takes one sideways step, release all pressure.

Try doing this exercise facing a wall or fence so that your horse cannot move forward. This will help the horse figure out what you are trying to do.

Teaching the Basic Cues through Air Pressure

When using air pressure, the idea is to signal with your body language. As a last resort you may have to use direct pressure. This mimics horses out in the field who will pin their ears to move another horse, then purse the lips, lower the head, step forward, open the mouth, and finally will bite if the horse they are trying to move still has not gotten the hint.

You want to progress the same way, making sure that you are consistent every time for the same cue, getting more intense and clear with your instructions if the horse does not respond. Be sure to progress fairly quickly through the intensities of the cue until you get what you want.

As soon as you get a step in the right direction BACK OFF and either stop asking completely if you get the desired reaction, or if you want a few more steps or a faster response then back off by going back down to a less intense cue—perhaps going back to your ideal cue and wait for the response you want.

Remember to evaluate the situation and make sure that what you are asking is fair considering the training level, the environment, the fitness of the horse, the relationship, and the segment in your training session.

Move Forward

Steps to get a horse moving forward using pressure behind the horse:

1. Stand beside your horse. Hold your rope in the hand closest to his head. Hold your stick in the hand closest to the hind. Stand about 3 to 5 feet away from the horse, next to his barrel (the riding position). Rest your stick on the horse's back where the riding position is.

2. Move your stick behind the horse and motion the stick up and down. If the horse does not respond then slap the stick (or rope on the end of the stick) on the ground. If the horse still does not respond than tap him just above the tail.

3. As soon as the horse moves forward return the stick to neutral position, resting the stick on his back where the riding position is.

The idea is not to hurt the horse when tapping with the string or with the stick, but instead to make it uncomfortable and encourage the horse to think 'How can I get her to stop flicking that string at me?' There is a difference between making a situation uncomfortable, and making a situation painful.

Sending Forward

1. You can see Lindsey using her ideal cue to send Thetis forward. Lindsey's stick and string are resting on Thetis's back where the riding position is. You can see that Thetis has started to walk forward, so Lindsey did not need to increase the cue (or she would have had to lift her stick and fling the string behind Thetis).

2. Lindsey has asked Thetis to halt and is giving her a rub with the stick. This allows Thetis time to think about the cue and it reminds her that the tools are friendly.

3. Lindsey has sent Thetis up into trot and you can see Thetits trotting. Thetis is also asking Lindsey a question - you can see Thetis has flicked her ear closest to Lindsey, towards Lindsey. Thetis's raised head set shows that she is not as comfortable with this exercise at the trot as she is at the walk.

If your horse starts to show signs of panic or anxiousness like a raised head paired with quick choppy movement, or wide eyes with a tense expression, then do not use any more pressure—instead use less pressure. You want to keep your horse in the thinking logical mode and away from the fight-or-flight mode.

Trouble Shooting:

The horse may not be paying attention when you do the ideal cue—no problem! It is the horse's responsibility to pay attention to you. You ask, and if the horse misses the ideal cue from lack of attention, he will start to learn to watch you more carefully and be more attentive looking for those ideal cues.

Move Backward

Steps for moving a horse backward using air pressure:

1. Stand in front of your horse with the halter on and lead rope in hand, facing him.

2. Start with your ideal cue, which for many is waving your finger at your horse, almost like shaking a finger saying 'no.' The finger shaking should be the same hand holding the rope. The other hand is still at your side resting on the stick. Wave your finger at the horse for less than a minute, then advance to wiggling the rope, advancing to a hard wiggle in the rope, then advancing to a full arm wiggling on the rope so that your lead rope snap bumps the horse in the chin, simulating a nip. Keep the wiggle going and pick up the stick if needed and fling the string toward the horse's chest for added pressure (this will take some coordination, and you may want to practice without a horse first).

3. As soon as the horse takes a step back you should stop and wait for the horse to lick his lips and digest the thought for a couple minutes, or however long it takes for your horse to digest a thought. Do this a couple of times until you only have to move to a light wiggle in the rope to back the horse, and then move on to something else.

Practice this every play session in short bursts (just 2 to 3 backups) and eventually your horse will just move backward off of the shaking of the finger. Keep in mind that if you ask over and over again for your horse to back up, he may think he is doing something wrong and will start trying something else.

After your horse understands this concept, you can now back him up by standing at any angle (the side of the horse, behind, at the shoulder, etc.) and wiggle the rope to back up. This means less pulling on the horse, which means less 'trapping-like behaviour.' Instead of bumping the rope, do a wiggle to stop and back up your horse.

Backing Up with Air Pressure

Above:
Lindsey gives Thetis her ideal cue to have her back up

Left:
Lindsey has to increase intensity because Thetis has not backed up

Right:
Lindsey increases intensity of the cue again by wiggling the rope up and down to tell Thetis to back up

It is important to teach the wiggle in the rope so you can back your horse up when holding the lead rope, but it's equally important to teach him to back up using the stick. This is because if you plan to play at liberty you will not have a rope to wiggle, and also it is important to teach that the stick is used for all cues. To do this, follow these directions:

You can try starting with your ideal cue, but instead of a wiggle in the rope you can shake your stick up and down at the horse. Advance to tapping the ground and even advance to tapping the horse, or tagging him with the string (depending on how close he is to you) until he backs up.

Trouble Shooting:

It is very common for four things to happen when doing this:

1) **The horse starts walking forward.** In this case you should shake the rope harder, add the pressure from the stick, and keep asking until he backs up. If you are worried about the horse walking into you then you are not standing your ground strongly enough, and perhaps you should stand on the other side of a fence/partition to give you more confidence, or have someone help you.

2) **The horse has his head turned away from you.** This is a sign of lack of confidence. Turn your belly button away from your horse and he will usually look straight at you again. This is a sign that the horse has respect, but is not yet connected enough with you to give you two eyes because he finds you have too much pressure in your stance and/or presence.

3) **The horse is not paying attention when you shake your finger.** No problem! It is the horse's responsibility to pay attention to you. You ask your ideal cue, and if the horse misses the ideal cue from lack of attention, then just progress to the higher cue intensity (in this case a wiggle in the rope). Eventually the horse will start to learn to watch you more carefully and be more attentive in looking for those ideal cues.

4) **You end up teaching your horse an ideal cue that you didn't mean to.** This is because many people will fumble with the rope before raising their finger (with the rope in hand) to shake and ask the horse to back up. Some horses will learn that the fumbling of the rope is the ideal cue and will start to back up when you do this. Do not punish the horse for this—the horse is right. Instead you need to practice being more careful with the rope, or turn away from your horse while you are preparing your tools.

Come

This cue teaches you to draw the horse toward you. It is easiest if you practice this with back up.

1. Start by either backing your horse up about 5 to 10 feet, or by positioning yourself 5 to 10 feet away from your horse.

2. Ask with your ideal cue for the horse to come (this could be motioning with your hand, patting your leg, tilting backward, etc.). Reinforce the cue with a pleasant and relaxed posture and facial expression, backing up a step, and then if needed you can draw the horse toward you with the rope by wheeling the rope in. Start with light pressure on the rope and increase pressure until the horse comes forward.

3. Release tension with every step forward the horse takes toward you.

Trouble Shooting:

Sometimes the horse will turn his head from you. This is a sign that he lacks confidence, or he'll be reluctant to come toward you. If this happens, analyze your posture and expression. You want to appear inviting. Have a happy facial expression and relaxed stance. You don't want to look like you are standing your ground—you want to signal to the horse that it is okay to approach you. You can make your space more inviting by turning a leg outward, pointing your belly button away from the horse, and/or by taking a step backward when the horse does eventually step toward.

Haunch Turn (move your front end)

This cue is more difficult and I recommend doing this one after you have established that your horse truly understands moving from direct pressure and air pressure for the other cues. Also making sure you have a good back up will help with this cue.

1. Stand on either side of your horse, just in front of the shoulder. Hold your stick in the hand farther from the horse's body, while standing facing the direction you will be walking (so you will be facing the same way as the horse). Your rope will be in the hand closest to the horse.

2. Lead your horse forward. Use the stick and string to fling behind you if the horse is lagging behind.

3. Practice turns by waving the stick in circles to give the cue to move the front end. Keep the stick right near the front of the horse because you want the pressure from the stick to say two things: 1) move the front end, and 2) don't go forward. Depending on how sharp a turn you want to make will depend on how much you angle your stick in front of the horse. You want your stick at the side of the horse's face and angled in front of his nose. Use the wiggle in the rope to slow the horse down if needed. If your horse is not responding to the circling stick, try two circles in the air and then the next circle tap the hair on the horse's face, and then do another two circles with the stick in the air and the next circle touch the hair a little harder. Be sure to be still (which is the reward) when the horse moves away from the pressure.

4. After a few turns when your horse is getting the concept, ask for sharper turns, and then try doing a haunch turn from the halted position (this is harder because you don't have momentum).

Haunch Turn Using Air Pressure

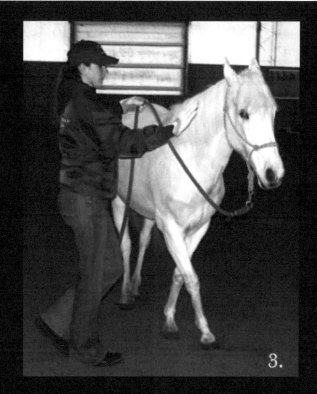

3.

1.

2.

1. Lindsey is using her stick in a tapping motion to ask Ellie to complete the haunch turn by moving her front end. Notice how Lindsey has the rope in her left hand.

2. Lindsey continues the haunch turn in the same direction, but now uses the stick in a circular motion, so she has swapped her rope to her right hand. You can see Ellie stepping out to the side with her right front hoof, and you can see her right hind hoof firmly planted in the ground.

3. Lindsey now has dropped her stick entirely and is just using her hand to create air pressure, asking Ellie to complete the haunch turn going the opposite way. You can see Ellie crossing her front legs nicely to complete the turn.

Next steps:

1. Stand about 5 to 10 feet away from your horse, just in front of the shoulder. Face his shoulder. Hold the stick in the hand closest to the shoulder and the rope in the hand closest to the head of the horse.

2. Start by asking with your ideal cue. This can be by resting the stick against your side and using your hand in a wave-like motion at the horse suggesting to move the shoulder, or your ideal cue can be using the stick in a wave-like (up & down) motion at the shoulder/neck area asking the horse to move the front end. If the horse does not move the front end, then reinforce with the stick in a circular motion, tagging on the neck if the horse is not responding. Be sure to be still when the horse moves correctly, as this is the reward. Allow enough time for the horse to digest this thoroughly (usually a minute) before you ask again.

3. When the horse moves you should walk in the direction you want him to move, keeping your belly button pointing in the direction you want to go.

Remember that in order for the horse to move the front end only, he'll be moving in a circle with the front end, so you will have to walk accordingly (meaning you will also have to walk in a big circle—it is not possible for the handler to stay walking in a straight line).

Trouble Shooting:

It is common for horses to walk forward or even get a bit quick sometimes when first teaching this cue. Make sure your horse understands your tools are friendly, and the wiggle to back up, because you are dealing with a sensitive pressure zone (the head, eyes, and ears). Be quick to correct by wiggling the rope to back the horse up for any forward steps. **Ask for one step at a time.**

What if your horse runs from the stick? Then you need to go back to the basics and teach your horse that your tools are friendly by rubbing your horse all over with the sticks, flinging the stick around without harmful intention and not directed toward the horse, and only stopping when the horse is still.

Forehand Turn (move your haunches)

This is one of the easiest basic cues you can do, and my favourite to use with a 'hot' horse or one in fight-or-flight mode.

Steps to doing a forehand turn using air pressure:

1. Stand 5 to 10 feet away from your horse, holding the rope in the hand closest to the horse's head, and the stick in the opposite.

2.   Progress through your cues. Your ideal cue can be to crouch down a LITTLE bit and intently look at the side of the horse's rear—the same way horses do in the field as their warning (except you can't pin your ears!). Keep the rope to the horse fairly short so that you can pull his head towards you if needed.

3.   After crouching and looking at the hind end, if the horse moves the hind end as asked, then stand up in relaxed posture and be still to reward the horse. If not, then raise your stick pointing to the hind end, then motion the stick at the hind end, and if the horse still isn't moving the hind end, then tag the side of the horse near the hind end. Be careful not to aim your pressure too far back on the horse or he may think you are sending him forward. Be ready to pull his head toward you if he tries to run off, or wiggle the rope if he moves forward.

4.   Stand up with a relaxed posture, with the stick at your side. As soon as the horse moves the hind end away from you, do nothing, as a reward to the horse.

Trouble Shooting:

The first few times you do this, the horse may run forward, in which case you should continue to ask him to yield the hind end, but with less pressure, and be quick to wiggle the rope to stop him from going forward. Reward the horse for the right answer by standing still, with relaxed posture, and the stick at your side. Allow the horse enough time to digest the thought (look for the horse chewing his lips, lowering his head, or letting out a sigh). If you are unsure if your horse is finished digesting a thought, then wait two or three more minutes to be sure the horse has had ample time to think about your communication. **Remember to be consistent with your cues.**

Facing Up

Facing up is a cue you use to ask the horse to stop, turn and face you. This is something you use to get your horse's attention, prepare to ask a new cue, or to use as a signal to the horse that he has finished the task you wanted and now he can just face up. Facing up can be very helpful when you start to play with your horse without any halter or rope attached. This is because if the horse starts to walk away or get distracted, you can simply face up your horse.

Steps to facing up a horse

1. Start by holding the rope in the hand closest to the horse's head and the stick in the hand closest to the hind end. Stand facing the horse.

2. Start with your ideal cue, which should be a crouch directed at the horse's hind end. Some people may just tilt their head, others bend so far over that it looks like they are bowing to the horse. Do whatever works for your cues and personality—just be consistent with your ideal cue (ask the same each time).

3. If the horse does not respond then raise up the stick, give it a little twirl, and then tag the horse with the stick/string on the hind end if the horse still has not responded. This entire progression of cues should happen in less than 30 seconds. When you tag the horse be ready to pull his head toward you to help him figure out what you are saying.

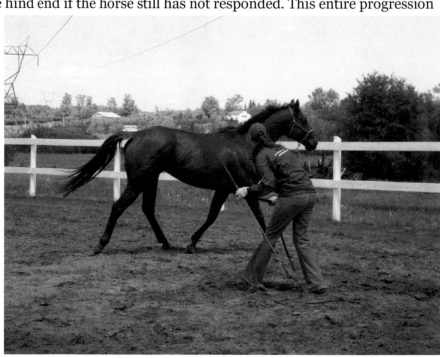

4. As soon as the horse turns and faces you, stand up and be still with a relaxed posture and the stick at your side. This is the reward for the horse. Allow a few minutes pause.

You can also then draw the horse toward you by backing up when he faces you. Backing up will take any pressure off the horse and will cause him to walk toward you. If your horse's body is facing you, but his head is turned away, this means he's being respectful but is still not 100 percent confident. Try standing with your belly button pointing away from the horse. This will remove some pressure that the horse may be feeling and he should then be able to look at you.

Trouble Shooting:

Sometimes horses can get a bit quick when first teaching face up because the progression of cues is quick, and the whole movement is fairly quick. Be careful to have the rope short enough that you can easily pull the horse's head toward you. This will help your communication to be very clear. Once the horse has faced up a couple times, you will likely not have to pull the head toward you.

This cue differs from the forehand turn because the horse will move the hind so that he faces you—whereas for the forehand turn the horse moves so that they pivot on a front foot. Generally, for facing up, you crouch/bend over a bit more. For the forehand turn you stand up a bit straighter and create great pressure by walking at the horse with your belly button and both eyes on the horse.

Sideways

Before you attempt to teach sideways from air pressure, you need to check your basic cues. Can you move the front end, can you move the back end, can you wiggle to stop, and can you move forward? Can you do all of these cues from five feet or more away from your horse? If you answered no to any of these, you need to slow down and go back to that cue and practice a few more times.

Start by practicing against a fence or arena wall so your horse's only options are sideways or backing up. Keep yourself right at the fence/wall, even if the horse backs up, because you do not want to create a gap where the horse can go forward and in front of you. Once your horse can move sideways about 10 or more feet along an arena wall or fence, then you can try without the guide wall.

Steps to doing sideways from air pressure:

1. Start by facing your horse's side and standing 5 to 10 feet away. There are two main ways to teach this.

A) Ask the horse to move the front end a step, then ask him to move the back end by using the stick (do not crouch, just point the stick at the hind end and move it the same as you do the front end). Then move back to the front end and then move the hind end. Take pauses as your horse moves, wiggling to correct if the horse goes forward or putting pressure behind if the horse backs up. Continue until your stick is swaying right to left and your horse figures out to move sideways.

    The idea is that you move the front end one step, then the back end, then the front end, etc. until your horse realizes it would just be easier to move sideways and he offers to move sideways. The ideal is to get a single motion of swaying the stick right to left (or swaying your hand right to left) asking for sideways. You can also use this method of moving the front and then moving the back end by swinging the string in circular motions, hitting the ground, and potentially tagging the horse if the horse does not move.

B) The other main way to ask is to use the rope in one hand to fling toward the horse's shoulder asking him to move the front end, and using the stick to move the back end, so that you are asking both ends at the same time to achieve sideways. I do not recommend this way because ideally you want to be able to move the horse without using the rope, and also because sometimes the horse may get confused with the rope being used at the front end and may back up.

Sideways using Air Pressure

1. Sending Thetis to the wall 2. Asking for sideways 3. Thetis isn't paying attention so Lindsey taps her belly to increase the cue intensity 4. A rewarding pause 5. & 6. Sideways the other way

1.

4.

2.

5.

3.

6.

2. For both methods, as soon as the horse takes a step in the right direction, stop, be still, be relaxed, and just rest the stick at your side. Allow time for the horse to digest the thought.

Trouble Shooting:

Sometimes horses will get confused and signals will get mixed up because the handler is standing too close to the horse. This is because if you stand too close to the horse (within five feet) he can't easily see the cues you're using. The result is that you end up doing more cues with direct pressure rather than air pressure. Keep yourself at least five feet away from the horse.

Horses will be searching for the comfort and may try to go forward. This means if you leave a gap between you and the wall, the horse may try to go forward and in between you and the wall to complete a circle. Be careful not to allow the horse to go between you and the wall.

Sometimes horses will get stuck on the wall, meaning the horse will stand at the wall/fence and won't move in any direction. Try starting with your horse about ten feet from the wall. You stand at the wall. Send your horse to the wall by getting the horse to walk forward. Use that forward energy to help the horse move sideways because the horse is already moving. This means you will start to ask for sideways while your horse is still moving forward toward the wall. It is best to let the horse take three to four steps forward toward the wall, and then start asking for sideways when the horse still has three to four steps of room to move forward. This will help the horse figure out what you want. Be sure to practice both sides!

Round Abouts

A round about is similar to lunging except you don't follow the horse with your eyes or your stick. The horse will circle around you as you stand still in the middle of the circle, passing the rope behind your back. You trust your horse to complete the circle and continue in the same direction in the same gait. Parelli terms this 'circling'. The round about has many purposes that lunging cannot teach. It teaches the horse his responsibilities, which will translate into riding.

The responsibilities of the horse include:

1) The horse needs to watch where he is going. He learns this because you will not steer him around obstacles or coach him over poles.

2) The horse must keep going in the same direction until asked otherwise. You teach this by correcting right away if the horse switches direction. By allowing the horse to make the mistake, you can then correct him and teach that it is his responsibility to keep going the same way, rather than you having the responsibility to continuously nag the horse to go in one direction.

3) The horse learns to maintain speed because you will correct him when he falls out of gait. To start with, only correct when the horse falls out of gait—do not be picky about the speed of the gait.

Round About

1. Sending out on the round about with the ideal cue   2. Sending out on the round about with slightly increased intensity, but still not using the stick
3. Circling on the round about   4. Disengaging from the round about

Round Abouts Teach Your Horse:

- to keep the same pace

- to stay the same direction

- to watch where they are going

Once you have practiced several times and your relationship is ready for more criticism, you control the speed within the gait (collected walk, trot/jog, canter/lope, etc).

4) The horse maintains trust in the relationship by keeping it a partnership. Because you will not be watching and following the horse around in circles with a whip pointed at the haunches, the round about helps solidify your partnership relationship and takes you away from having a prey and predator relationship.

Your horse will also learn the 'send', which will be useful when jumping, doing free work, and when getting creative asking for other advanced cues and tricks.

Steps to the round about using air pressure:

1. Start by backing your horse up to about 5 to 10 feet away. Stand facing your horse. Hold the rope in one hand with the stick resting at your hip in neutral (but be ready to pick it up).

2. Send your horse right or left by pointing your finger/hand/arm/body in the direction you want the horse to go (use whatever your ideal cue will be). If the horse does not leave to go in that direction, then reinforce by raising your stick (if you want the horse to go to the left, then you will raise the stick in the right hand, and vice versa for the other direction). Circle the stick the same way you do to move the front end, as your goal is to move the shoulder out, then add pressure behind the horse to send him forward. Tag the horse's hind end if necessary, or if he gets out of the way in time, you can tag the ground where he was standing.

3. The horse can head out on the round about at the walk or trot, but wiggle the rope to slow the horse down if the horse heads into a canter.

4. Have the horse do one to two circles and then face up the horse by crouching at the hind end, pulling the head toward you if needed.

5. Stand up with a relaxed posture when the horse faces you.

When your horse understands and can do one to two circles, try asking for two to three circles. Every time your horse turns to face you, what he's asking is, 'Shouldn't I be doing something else?' You should respond to your horse with the answer—to keep circling. Do this by starting back at the ideal cue (quickly—so as not to reward the horse by letting him stand for too long), but be sure to start at the ideal cue (you do not want to punish him for asking a question). It is quite nice for a horse to look to you for clarification rather than to run off, so be sure to respond kindly and patiently.

You should be passing the rope behind your back, not watching your horse except out of your peripheral vision. Listen to make sure the horse is still going; horses will often stand and face you behind your back because there is less pressure on your backside. When this happens just turn and face the horse, and start again at the ideal cue. Your horse will eventually understand that you do indeed just want him to keep going in a circle. Once you can complete three round abouts in each direction, and disengage your horse (face up the horse) easily by crouching at the hind end and having the horse face you, you are ready to move on.

Trouble Shooting:

If your horse runs to the end of the rope and bumps himself on the rope causing him to stop, reinforce with the stick behind the horse to move him forward.

If your horse leaves very sluggishly, use the stick and string to tag the exact spot where he's standing when you gave your ideal cue. Do this within 3 to 5 seconds of giving your ideal cue. This means that if your horse leaves sluggishly, then he'll get a tag on the rear, but if he leaves for the round about with more enthusiasm then the ground where he was standing will be tagged. You want to make the spot where he was standing uncomfortable, and motivate him to get out of that spot quickly after you give your ideal cue and higher intensity cues. The higher intensity cues are: 1) picking up the stick, 2) circling the stick, and 3) tagging with the string on the stick.

Step 3: Putting the Basic Cues to Work

It is important to put the basic cues to work so that you do not get 'stuck' in the basic cues and turn them into a horrible routine that your horse learns to dread. Once your horse has a pretty good understanding of a basic cue, put it to work to make it more interesting. To move on, your horse does not need to be moving off of ideal cues, but be sure that your horse does not need a high level of intensity in the basic cue before you move on. Often just from putting the cues to work your horse will start to move off the ideal cues because he becomes more interested in what it is you are doing. Remember the idea is to keep the horse thinking and to use communication with the horse. This means you want to keep trying new things and testing the language you have together.

Ideally you don't want to use your rope unless you have to. If you can work your horse as if you have no rope halter and lead (using only your body language and your stick/string), then you are better prepared to do freedom (liberty) work with no halter and rope because you can still communicate with your horse. You should practice on line and then test at liberty (freedom work). This means that when you are playing with your horse using your rope and halter, you are practicing cues and games that you can later try during freedom work (no halter or rope).

When advancing out of a basic cue into something more advanced, you need to check your ingredients. When you check your ingredients, you are simply checking that your horse has a working concept of the basic cue. So when you ask a horse to back up with air pressure, if he moves forward or requires a really high level of intensity (such as tagging the horse) to get the horse to back up, then you need to work on this before you can proceed with the advancement. If your horse hesitates and requires a stronger wiggle in the rope, but then backs up a few steps, you are ready to advance with the cue. An ingredient for all cues and games should be 'my tools are friendly.' If your horse is scared of your tools then you must first desensitize your horse before you can proceed.

Follow Me

Cues: Go forward and back up. For advanced follow me you need all the basic cues.

You can play follow me in many variations. You can have your horse follow you, halt and back up with you. You can also advance the game to include walking sideways with you, walking in a haunch or forehand turn, or going over a jump or pole together. Start with the simple cues and progress as you gain more experience with your horse to include sideways and other more difficult cues.

Steps to follow me:

1. Start by standing beside your horse. Hold the lead rope in the hand closest to the horse and the stick in the hand further from the horse. You should be facing forward in the direction you will be walking. Your belly button should always point in the direction you want to go.

2. Start walking. If the horse falls behind then use your stick and string to tag behind you while you keep looking and walking forward. Keep the lead rope short enough so that you can direct your horse. The idea is for the horse to follow at the shoulder or slightly in front of the shoulder at your side.

3. Stop. To stop your horse, first stop your own feet, then pick up your stick, and hold it in front of the horse to put pressure in front of the horse to stop (only pick the stick up if your horse didn't stop when you did). Wiggle the rope if needed to get the horse stopped.

4. Back up. Start backing up yourself, still facing forward, and use your stick to put pressure in front of the horse. Wiggle the rope if needed.

5. Walk forward again, tagging behind if needed.

6. Go forward into the trot, tagging behind if needed.

   If your horse has a working understanding of yielding the front end, the back end or sideways then you can turn into your horse, either left or right, to incorporate these basic cues into follow me. The objective is for you to stay at the shoulder of the horse so that you and the horse are glued together as a pair working in harmony. You want to only use your stick and body language if possible so that you can then test this by doing freedom work and trying it without a rope or halter. Only use the rope if absolutely needed.

Transitions on the Round About (teaching walk/trot/canter/halt/back up)

Cues: Round about, disengage (face up), send, go forward and stop/back up.

Steps to working with transitions on the round about:

1. Start by sending your horse onto the round about. Most horses will leave at the walk or trot.

2. Ask your horse to go one gait faster (so if the horse is in the walk, send him into the trot). First send the horse by pointing in the direction you want to go, then reinforce by raising the stick and putting pressure behind the horse, tagging the ground behind him, or the horse himself if needed. Do not be picky about the speed within the gait; at this stage in your relationship only determine the gait itself (walk, trot, canter, halt, and back up). Once you have perfected your transitions and can achieve all gaits, you can get pickier about doing a slow or fast gait.

3. To slow or stop your horse, first pick up the stick and point it in front of the horse. Fling the string in front of the horse if needed, and add wiggle to the rope if needed. Do the same for back up, but with a bit more movement from the stick than when you are slowing the horse down. If the horse turns to face you, he's asking a question. Respond by politely yielding the front end back out on the circle.

Start by only asking for transitions within one gait/gear of the horse. So, for example, if your horse is walking then you can ask him to either stop or trot. Once you have perfected these transitions you can ask him to move through two gears—for example, asking the horse to go from a walk to a canter. To do this, try making your ideal cue slightly different/more intense than when moving through only one gear. Some people also develop vocal cues to assist the body language, such as making a clicking or clucking noise to trot, making a kiss noise to canter, saying 'whoa' to stop, saying 'easy' to slow down, and saying 'back' to back up. Vocal commands can help a horse, but be sure that you are still using body language and can go through the transitions with just body language.

Being able to move your horse through the transitions with body language further develops your language with the horse. This will enable you to do more advanced or complex tasks in the future and will also help you fine tune your language so you understand the pressure areas on the horse. This means you can figure out your horse's level of sensitivity. For example, you can discover how much pressure it takes for the horse to go forward: one gear versus two. You can also discover the different pressure points on the horse. For example, you can learn the difference between sending your horse on the circle, versus putting pressure in front of the horse causing him to stop/slow. You will also get better at sending the pressure in the right spot to either face up the horse, or to send the horse forward.

The 'gears' on a horse in order are: back up, halt (stop), walk, trot, canter, gallop.

Transitions on a Round About

1. Walking online on a round about 2. Sending into trot online on a round about
3. Sending into trot at liberty on a round about with an increased intensity cue
4. Sending into canter at liberty on the round about with an ideal cue

Go Through Something (the basic step before trailering)

Cues: Send, move forward, move the front end.

Set up something for your horse to go between—perhaps two barrels, two buckets, a log and tree, two jump standards, two poles parallel to each other, etc. Start with objects that are fairly far apart—about five to seven feet. As your horse is more comfortable, you can make the objects closer and closer together, perhaps even close enough so that your horse has to jump the objects rather than go between them.

For this exercise you want to make sure your horse is comfortable working in a circle fairly close to you. To determine your horse's comfort level follow this simple exercise:

1. Start by standing about ten feet from a wall or fence (not an electric or wire fence).

2. Send your horse on a round about so that the horse has to go between you and the fence/wall. Remember to send by using your ideal cue (whether it's a finger point, full arm pointing, etc.) in the direction you want the horse to go, then reinforce by raising your stick, waving the stick, and finally tagging the horse if he's giving no effort. Recognize that a horse stretching out his neck, looking warily at the space, IS an effort. Stepping on the spot, contemplating going forward IS an effort, but standing still with no movement and with no curiosity IS NOT an effort.

3. Disengage your horse after he goes through the space (have the horse turn and face you by putting pressure on the hind end, and then allow a pause for the horse to digest the thought).

4. Only add more pressure if the horse is giving NO effort—even if he's just looking, leave him alone. If the horse starts to back up or tries to change direction, be sure to have the lead rope at a length where you can direct the horse's head in the direction you want by pulling on the rope, or pushing with the stick. If the horse is close enough to you that tagging with the rope is impractical, then tap with your stick behind the horse or on his bum only hard enough to cause a response. The intent is only to show him that standing still doing nothing is uncomfortable, and to motivate him to look for comfort. Never whip your horse.

5. Move closer to the fence/wall and repeat the steps above. Send the horse through the space between you and the wall. Do this in both directions.

6. Do these steps to determine how narrow a space your horse will go between. If your horse has hesitancy going between you and a wall five feet away, then you can imagine that going into a trailer space might be even more difficult. Play this game occasionally to check where your horse's comfort level is with you. You should be able to send your horse through a space of about four feet between you and a wall before proceeding to trailering.

7. Set up two objects with a space between them of about five to seven feet. Stand about ten feet from the object and send your horse between the objects following the directions above. Be careful to remember to keep the horse facing the space, and add pressure when the horse is not giving a forward effort.

8. Disengage the horse and be still with a relaxed posture, asking for nothing as soon as your horse does the correct thing—this is the reward to the horse.

Practicing sending your horse through objects will set you up nicely for trailering because you will have taught your horse the routine of sending between objects. An excellent test before you get to a trailer is to put two poles parallel to each other, about three feet apart, with a tarp underneath the poles. Send your horse through the poles. Once he's comfortable with this, try to send him through the poles and stop him before he exits the poles/leaves the tarp. This way you have established that you can send him into a narrow space with a funny sounding floor. You can also use a sheet of plywood to walk over, a shower curtain, or garbage bags/feed sacks.

Remember the key to using your basic cues is to be creative and use change. You want to be careful that your horse does not fall into a routine of tricks and games. It is best to keep your horse thinking, and test your communication by asking for new things and using new objects and props.

Trailer Loading

Trailer loading can be a frustrating process. Trailer loading can also be a display of some interesting horse training techniques. I have heard stories and seen many different methods of loading horses onto trailers. These improper techniques include coaxing a horse onto a trailer with treats, blind folding the horse, using lunge lines around the horse's rump to pull him inside, hooking a horse up to a truck with a rope and pulling him on, whipping the horse onto the trailer, and many more bizarre, cruel, humiliating, and just plain wrong techniques for loading horses onto trailers.

Trailer loading is one of the more difficult things to teach a horse because of the horse's prey animal instinct. By nature the horse does not want to walk into a dark enclosed space with no exit. This is for the simple reason that the horse would not be able to run away from a predator.

A trailer is quite intimidating for a horse, so you need to take some steps to make your trailer as inviting as possible. The more inviting your trailer, the easier it will be to load your horse. Address the following trailer basics before you begin loading your horse:

1. **Use the biggest trailer you can**. You want a wide trailer that is tall enough for the horse you are using. A 7ft height inside the trailer or taller is a must for horses 16H or bigger. Stock trailers are great for ample space, but if you only have access to a trailer with dividers/stalls, try and take the partition out while loading to make the trailer more inviting.

2. **Have plenty of light**. Your horse will prefer loading into a well-lit trailer. Have windows uncovered and escape doors open (provided the horse is not at risk of going through the escape door). If it is dark out, then turn on trailer lights and use flashlights within the trailer.

3. **No clutter**. The trailer is scary enough without added objects within the trailer. Remove everything from the trailer that doesn't need to be there while loading. Once your horse is comfortable with the trailer, it will be unnecessary to remove everything—but be sure to limit clutter for safety reasons. When loading a horse you do not want yourself or your horse to get tangled or caught on anything. This includes having no animals lingering around the trailer.

4. **Get the humans to back away**. Any extra people around the trailer could make your horse nervous. It seems that when it comes to trailer loading, everyone wants to watch or give advice. However, you have to get all extra people to be a minimum of 10-20 feet away from the back of the trailer. Only the handler and possibly one assistant should be close to the trailer loading entrance and the horse. Everyone else needs to back away.

5. **Make it comfortable**. Bed your trailer with bedding your horse is familiar with. This means use the same shavings or straw that you use around the barn in the trailer. Be sure to use bedding in the trailer that is easy for your horse to stand on. You don't want your horse slipping about inside the trailer. Provide a hay bag or hay net with familiar hay. Once inside you can give your horse treats, but do not use treats to coax the horse onto the trailer.

6. **Use a step up**. Horses generally prefer loading onto step up trailers instead of ramp loading trailers. This is because a horse is more stable when stepping up into a trailer than walking on a rubber-padded ramp. Horses may slip on the ramp and this can cause the horse to fear the trailer. If you are using a ramp, be sure the surface is dry, free of manure, and free of material the horse can slip on.

The next thing you have to do is have appropriate tools. Make sure you have the following:

- A rope halter

- A 12 foot lead rope with heavy snap

- An arm extension stick with a string attached

- Appropriate trailering bandaging or protective wear for the horse

- A lunge line or a long rope

Now that you have everything prepared, you are ready to practice moving your horse with direct pressure to establish your leadership and language. The most important basic cues to practice are moving forward and moving the front end (haunch turn). You should practice around the trailer, so that your horse understands that your relationship and language are priorities even when a trailer is present. Once your horse is responding to the basic cues fairly easily, you are ready to trailer load.

Follow these steps for trailer loading:

1. Start by double-checking that your horse understands that your tools are friendly. Rub the lunge lines, arm extension stick, and lead rope over the horse.

2. Walk towards the trailer. If the horse hesitates, allow the horse to slow down, but keep the horse facing the trailer, and remember that once pressure is applied to the horse you must keep pressure on the horse until you get the response you want. This is because the reward is in the release. It is vital that you do not give up or send mixed signals. You would send mixed signals by asking the horse to go forward when putting pressure on the rope and halter, but then allowing slack in the rope before the horse gives you the response you want. Your process for cues will be:

   1) You start walking toward the trailer.

   2) If the horse is not walking beside you, then you will apply gentle pressure to the halter by pulling on the lead rope.

   3) If the horse still is not walking then you can apply a little more pressure on the rope.

   4) If the horse still is not walking forward then use your extension stick to tap the horse gently at the back of its rump (pressure behind the horse sends them forward). You could also tap a specific back leg to ask it to move forward. You will add intensity with the stick and string until the horse moves forward. You will be careful to do this while keeping pressure on the halter and rope.

   5) As soon as the horse steps forward you will release all pressure. You will not add pressure again until your horse signals they are comfortable. Signs that your horse is comfortable include: a relaxed head posture, relaxed ears or ears flicking toward you asking a question, your horse looking at you asking a question, resting a leg, and/or no signs of curiosity looking into the trailer, nor any signs of fear (fight-or-flight mode).

An important part of trailer loading is: ***do not ask for more, when your horse is already trying***. A second piece to this concept is to recognize that ***a horse being curious about the trailer is a horse trying***. This is important because a horse may stand for several minutes sniffing the trailer or ramp, and the horse may reach their head into the trailer looking around. It is important to recognize that this is the horse trying to confront their fear of the trailer and checking things out. If you add more pressure to the horse at this time, the horse is likely to go shooting backwards, not forwards, and even worse you will be severely damaging the relationship with your horse.

Do not add any pressure until your horse has stopped showing any signs of trying for about a minute. An experienced natural horseman may wait less than a minute of no trying before adding pressure, but until your ability to read a horse's body signals is excellent it is better to give your horse ample time to be curious, than to risk adding more pressure too soon.

Once you have reached the trailer, you may decide to proceed to loading, or you may decide to do middle steps. Some horses are so fearful of trailers, that middle steps are required. A middle step could be:

- Asking a horse to walk across the ramp of a trailer (from left to right, instead of straight into the trailer).

- Leading a horse to the trailer, allow the horse to sniff the trailer, and then lead the horse away from the trailer. Repeat until the horse can walk to the trailer confidently.

- Leading the horse to the trailer and then performing basic cues such as back up or a haunch turn when next to the trailer.

Not all horses require these middle steps, but depending on your horse's confidence level, your confidence level, and your competence level you may choose to take 5 minutes and complete a middle step or two. Once you have reached the trailer and are both calm and ready, it is time to move to the next step.

3. Stand at the side of the trailer and ask your horse to enter. You will stand at the side of the trailer because it is the safest place for you. Walking into a trailer with an anxious horse can be dangerous. It is best for you to stay outside the trailer. In addition, the horse will have to be on the trailer without a human for the trailer ride. This means that establishing from the start that the horse is to be comfortable on his own inside the trailer is beneficial. If your horse is fully comfortable inside the trailer, then you are less likely to have a horse pawing, kicking, or being restless during the trailer trip.

    Your main focus will be to keep the horse's head pointed into the trailer. Have your rope length short enough that you can direct the horse's head toward the trailer, without being so tight as to make the horse feel trapped which would get the horse more emotional.

    Now that you are at the trailer, the only pressure applied to the halter will be to keep the horse's head pointed into the trailer. Pressure to move the horse forward will come from behind the horse using your extension stick. There is already so much pressure in front of the horse (just with the tight trailer space), that adding any pressure to the halter to pull the horse forward would probably just send the horse shooting backwards.

You will use your extension stick as follows:

1. When the horse is no longer having any signs of trying (no sniffing, no checking out the trailer, etc.) you will gently tap at the back of the rump.

2. If the horse is still not moving forward after a few seconds, then increase the tapping until the horse starts trying again. Remember that this could be something as simple as the horse lowering his head and sniffing the ground.

3. Stop the pressure as soon as the horse starts trying.

4. Begin tapping when you are sure your horse is no longer trying.

The intent of the tapping is to encourage the horse to find comfort. This is done by making outside of the trailer uncomfortable, and making moving into the trailer comfortable. Moving into the trailer is comfortable because the tapping stops as soon as the horse moves forward or makes an effort to move forward. Being outside the trailer is uncomfortable because annoying tapping starts.

You should never tap your horse so hard that it could be considered beating or causing intense pain. However, when tapping a horse you should consider that horses are quite large strong animals and the average person is extremely unlikely to be able to tap a horse harder than horses kick each other at play when at liberty. Keep in mind that every horse is different. You should have a general understanding of how much pressure your horse can handle from doing the basic cues and other ground work up until this point.

The objective is to apply pressure that would make sense to the horse, but you can be creative about how you apply pressure. For sensitive horses this may be as simple as tapping the ground behind them, and for other horses you may tap behind their hind legs near the fetlocks (ankles).

Sometimes horses will swing their hind end around the side of the trailer making it hard for you to keep tapping them, yet the horse is no longer moving forward onto the trailer. When this happens you need some savvy to both keep your horse's head pointed into the trailer, and using your string attached to your stick to give you more reach to continue tapping the horse. When you lack the coordination, it might be easier to have an assistant. Your assistant can help you by standing with a lunge line that is attached to the back of the trailer creating a wall:

1) The lunge line attaches to the back of the trailer on the side opposite to the side that the handler is standing at. For example, if the handler is standing on the left side of the trailer, then the lunge line would attach to the right side of the trailer.

2) The assistant then walks backwards away from the trailer until they are at the end of the lunge line (any closer would put too much pressure on the horse and/or put the assistant in

danger from being kicked or trodden). This lunge line creates a wall preventing the horse from turning its body around the trailer. This helps keep the horse straight so the handler can continue.

Be persistent and patient during this process. Most horses that are generally considered horrible trailer loaders will load within 20 minutes. Horses that have had past bad experiences may take 30 minutes or longer. Be confident in yourself and continue keeping the cues and method the same until the horse loads.

After your horse loads, wait, allow the horse to fully back off the trailer, and then ask the horse to load onto the trailer again. This is an important last step. Most people will quickly hook up the tail bar and close the trailer door the second the horse has loaded. This is damaging because now your horse feels tricked, trapped, and emotionally the horse has not entered the trailer. Allowing your horse to back off the trailer fully and reloading will establish trust. You will make it your horse's idea to stay on the trailer because you will just keep reloading until your horse thinks 'hmm I might as well just stay on this thing.' Then your horse will stand quietly in the trailer and you can close up the trailer.

After your horse has loaded the first time, reloading should take less than a couple minutes for the average horse. Each time will likely be easier and easier. Most horses will decide to stay on the trailer after about 5-7 reloads, but some horses may take longer.

The benefits to practicing this step include:

- Having a horse stand quietly on the trailer

- Maintaining your partnership relationship with your horse

- Having a calmer horse upon arrival to wherever you are going

Once your horse is loaded and standing quietly, you can offer him treats. You want the trailer to be a comfortable and happy place. Providing some favourite treats can help make the trailer a happy place. People with their own trailers may even load the horse onto the trailer simply to feed the horse its afternoon meal, and then unload and turn him back out in the paddock.

Just remember that you cannot use treats to coax a horse onto a trailer. This is because if a horse's primary concern is safety then it means food will not work. If the horse loads with treats then it means the horse has trained you to fetch him treats meaning you are not the leader.

Trouble Shooting:

Most problems with trailer loading happen because the handler does not reward all the horse's efforts to go into the trailer. Recognize that a horse stretching out his neck, looking warily at the

Trailer Loading

1. Leading Cooper to the trailer

2. Lindsey allows Cooper to inspect the trailer

3. He resists going forward and pulls back and off to the side

4. Lindsey keeps constant pressure until Cooper gives forward

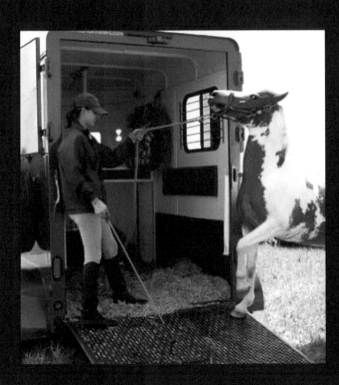

5. Lindsey has an assistant add a lunge line to create a wall (on the right)

6. Now Cooper cannot swing his hind around the trailer making it easier to ask him to load

7. Cooper starts to get curious about the trailer and reaches in

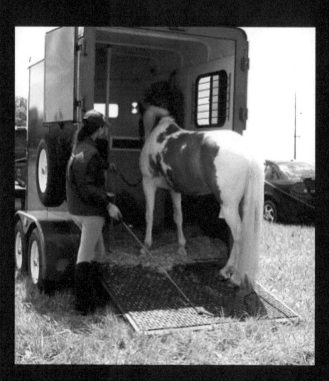

8. Once loaded, Lindsey gives Cooper a friendly rub and leaves the trailer door open

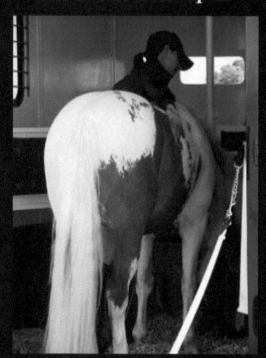

space, IS an effort. Stepping on the spot, contemplating going forward IS an effort. Standing still with no movement and no curiosity IS NOT an effort.

Other problems related to trailer loading come from lack of confidence in the handler. Ten minutes standing at the side of the trailer trying to load the horse can feel like an eternity and we often think that we might be doing something wrong. Most of the time the handler is doing the cues just right, but you just have to be patient.

Jumping (without a rider)

Steps to ask for jumping:

1. Set up a jump. When setting up a jump, make sure the jump is low enough that your horse is able to jump it and that there is no risk of your rope from getting caught on the jump.

2. Send your horse on a round about with the jump in the path. This way your horse will go over the jump in order to continue on the circular path.

3. If the horse stops at the fence, allow him to stop, but be sure he stays facing the fence. Then back him up and resend him over the fence. Keep resending the horse until he jumps the fence. Be sure that you are asking the horse with the right cues: Round about, move forward and disengage (face up). Jump a fair jump (suitable footing, appropriate height, the horse is sound and physically/mentally capable).

4. After the jump, disengage the horse so he knows he has done the correct thing.

There are two main ways to start a horse jumping on the ground. One is to place a pole on the ground and send the horse over the pole (follow the steps of the send in the 'round about' game, or in the 'go through something' game). As the horse gets comfortable, slowly raise the height of the jump. You can add placing poles, tunnels, and other props to help the horse get the correct striding and positioning over the jump.

The other way to start a horse jumping is to use two objects—for example, two barrels—that you first send your horse in-between. Then slowly move the objects closer and closer together until your horse has to jump because he can no longer fit in-between them.

You can get creative with jumping, even at low heights, by having your horse jump over things that have a different arrangement of objects underneath like pylons, coats, blankets, hay, feed bags, tarps, shower curtains, flowers, baskets, and more!

By jumping a variety of objects, even at low heights, you build the confidence of your horse and teach him to jump anything in sight. This is the first step to having an incredibly honest jumping horse that will not refuse anything.

A great reason to teach your horse jumping without a rider in the tack is because it allows the horse to learn how to jump without a rider getting in the way. Riders and tack can interfere with a horse's performance in many ways. The tack can be ill-fitting or constricting. The rider may alter the horse's balance by two pointing too soon or too late. The rider may yank on the horse's mouth or not allow enough of a release in the reins to allow the horse to jump with a rounded back.

A horse can sometimes take a bad jump to a fence, which can lower his confidence. When this happens you may have to lower the height of the fence to build back the horse's confidence. Allowing the horse to jump on his own can also build his confidence.

You can also do free jumping with your horse. Free jumping is an exercise in which you set up a jump beside a fence/wall in an enclosed space (so the jump is on the track/path of the ring) and send your horse around the ring, causing the horse to jump what is in his path. When free jumping, you can set up gymnastic exercises to teach your horse where to place his feet, to cause the horse to balance himself, and to help him be more athletic and use his body more efficiently.

Gymnastics for horses entails a combination of jumps of any height that contain distances of a bounce (land and jump another fence right away), one stride, two strides, or three strides in-between jumps. An athletic competition horse should be able to jump five jumps in a row, with bounce spacing, at a two foot height (depending on the horse's regular working height) with ease. Be sure to set distances of placing poles and jumps correctly or you may injure your horse.

You can also place guiding poles for horses to help them jump straight. Guiding poles (sometimes called tunnels) are simply poles on the ground on one or both sides of the jump, which the horse goes in-between. Horses that tend to drift to the left upon landing from the jump would benefit from a guiding pole placed on the left landing side of the jump.

Placing poles are poles placed either before the jump, after the jump, or on both sides. The placing pole helps the horse to find the correct take off and landing spots. You can use placing poles to help your horse space his striding correctly. You can do this by cantering/ trotting through poles placed at correct distances, place poles between jumps, or before/after jumps. Placing a pole a few feet from the jump's base encourages a horse to step over the pole and take off from the ideal spot. Putting poles between jumps helps a horse get the correct striding between fences. A horse that tends to take a long spot to the fence would benefit from a placing pole in front of the fence to encourage him to step deeper into the base of the fence.

You can also set up cross rails. Cross rails, also called X's, are jumps that have poles forming an X, which encourage a horse to jump the centre of the fence, which is the lowest point.

Jumping

1. A tire jump is good for learning horses because it can easily fall down and the rope is unlikely to get caught on it **2.** Jumping a cross-rail helps the learning horse to find the centre of the jump. Using a box instead of a standard on the one side means the rope is unlikely to get caught on the jump **3.** Jumping large solid fences is for experienced horses with good technique **4.** Barrels are a good introductory solid fence because they are not too big **5.** Free jumping

3.

1.

4.

2.

5.

Backing through Something

Cues: Back up, yield the front end, and yield the back end.

This is a great exercise to give you a clearer focus and give the horse a job. You can ask the horse to back through anything whether it is through a gate, exiting the arena, or through a set of pylons. When setting up a series of pylons or buckets, they can be in a straight line or crooked. You can start with three markers and advance from there as your horse and you understand the concept. Start with the markers fairly far apart—about 7 to 8 feet, and make them closer together as you get better.

The idea is to back your horse through the markers while staying at least five feet away from your horse, and never pulling the horse on the rope. Try to use your communication and test your signals. Use only your stick to motion the horse backward and yielding the front and hind ends. Take one step at a time.

Steps to backing through pylons:

1. Standing in front of your horse, or off to one side, at least five feet away.

2. First yield either the front or the back end of the horse to get the horse's hind end lined up with the space you are heading for.

3. Back the horse up, yielding the front or hind end as needed to keep the horse straight. Remember to pause and soften when the horse is correct.

4. Back up until you get through the pylon. Then redirect the horse's hind end by yielding the front and hind end as needed.

As your horse begins to understand the concept you can make the pause/reward less by making the break shorter and shorter until you can back through the pylons in a fluid motion.

You can also do this exercise using direct pressure, which is easier for most handlers when learning.

Bump Your Bum

Cues: Back up—it is easier if you can also yield the front and hind ends.

This exercise teaches you to back your horse up in a straight line. Simply set up one barrel or jump standard, or a dot on the wall.

Steps to bump your bum:

1. Start with your horse about five to ten feet away from the marker, and yourself standing about 5 to10 feet away from your horse.

Back through Something

Line up the horse to back through the gate

Using direct pressure to back the horse through the gate

Allowing the horse to have a reward by pausing, which gives the horse time to think

Bump Your Bum

Lindsey lines up Thetis to the post she is using as a marker to back towards

* is the post she is using as a marker

Lindsey starts to ask Thetis to back up

Thetis gets a bit crooked while backing up

Lindsey is able to straighten Thetis, so that she is nearly at the post

2. Ask your horse to back up using air pressure. When the horse gets crooked, straighten him by bumping the rope to the side or by using air pressure on whichever part of the horse needs to be lined up.

3. Keep backing up until the horse hits the marker with his bum.

This is a great exercise to get your horse and you to be more particular with your basic cues. Once you get more experienced with this game, you can start from farther away and use smaller markers.

Pole Bending (from the ground)

Cues: Yield the front end, send forward, and come.

Set up a series of barrels, jump standards (with the jump cups removed), pylons, or whatever markers you have. Put them in a straight line about 10 to 15 feet apart. Set up about 4 to 5 markers to start.

Steps to pole bending from the ground:

1. Start by picking a side (left or right) to stand beside your horse, and pick a side to stand on for the straight line of markers. If you stand on the left of your horse, then stand on the left of the markers as well. If you've chosen the left, stay on the left side of the markers for the whole exercise; it is your horse that will do the weaving through the markers, not the handler. Stand about 5 to 10 feet from your horse, in the riding position (just behind the shoulder), with enough room in the rope to allow the horse to go farther away from you when weaving.

2. Send the horse forward by pointing, and/or putting pressure behind him. Your objective is to get the horse walking forward so you can yield the front end more easily.

3. While the horse is walking forward, start yielding the front end with air pressure to send him through the opposite side of the marker, so that the marker is between you and the horse. Use air pressure and be sure to reinforce your cue with a tap of the stick if needed.

4. Once through the marker, draw the horse back toward you before the next marker by using your ideal cue for 'come' and pulling the lead rope if needed so that for the next marker you and the horse are on the same side again.

5. For the next marker yield your horse's front end out so the horse goes to the opposite side of the marker and the marker is between you and your horse.

6. Draw the horse back to you before the next marker so you and the horse are on the same side of the marker and finish with the horse at your side.

You can continue this pattern of weaving in and out of markers and advance this game by making the markers closer together, spread out in crooked lines, or by using different shapes or patterns. The objective of the markers is to help give you a focus when asking your horse to yield the front end, and give you an easy way to track your progress and challenge yourself.

Change Direction on the Round About

Cues: Round about, disengage, the send, slow/stop, yield the front end, yield the hind end

Steps to changing direction on the round about:

1. Send your horse out on a round about in an enclosed space, preferably a 60 feet diameter round pen, but a small paddock or arena will work; you just need to have a fence/wall that you can use.

2. Have your horse circle one to two times in the round about.

3. Ask for the change of direction by turning to face your horse, gathering up the rope (pulling the horse towards you as you do this) and back up towards the wall/fence.

4. Once the horse is walking towards you (you've achieved this by pulling the rope towards you and backing toward the wall), send the horse in the other direction by doing your ideal cue, and then reinforce with the stick if needed.

5. After the horse changes direction, have him circle one to two laps on the round about, then disengage and allow a rest for a reward.

From the steps above you will realize that the change of direction is two parts. The first is to draw the horse towards you by facing the horse and backing up; this allows you to then complete the second part, which is to send the horse in the opposite direction.

You can do this at the walk or trot to start—if you find it too quick at the trot then practice at the walk first. Once you are more coordinated and the horse gets the idea, you can advance to changing direction at the canter (which will sometimes get the horse to offer flying lead changes too). You can also advance this by doing changes of direction one after another, so that the distance between changes in direction is shorter (only let the horse go 10 to 15 feet before changing direction again); this will teach rollbacks and the beginnings of a spin.

Trouble Shooting:

If the horse runs past you, then back into the wall a little faster and collect the rope more quickly so that the horse is easier to stop/slow. Then send the horse in the other direction.

Keep your cues as subtle as you can. If there is too much movement the horse may get nervous and confused. When the horse does it correctly you can disengage and give him a break, or leave him alone on the round about for a lap or two.

Sideways Over a Pole

Cues: Sideways, stop/backup.

Steps to going sideways over a pole:

1. Start by putting a pole on the ground and walk your horse across the pole a couple of times to get him comfortable with the pole.

2. Lead your horse over the pole, stopping him with his front feet on one side of the pole and the hind feet on the other side. This means the pole will be underneath the horse and between the front legs and the hind legs.

3. ***Reward the horse*** by allowing him to walk off the poles, or just ***by standing still***.

4. Turn the horse around and revisit the pole, asking him to stand straddling the pole again.

5. Walk off again, turn back around, stopping straddling the pole again. Do this a couple of times to allow him to get comfortable stopping with something between his legs and underneath him. Horses are generally wary of something being underneath them because they're prey animals and like to keep everything where they can see it. They can't easily see the pole when it's underneath them, so building the confidence of the horse to accept this is necessary.

6. Now ask for sideways with direct pressure or air pressure (whichever you can do more easily—usually direct pressure). Do one sideways step at a time, pausing after each sideways step as a reward, until the horse has gone enough steps so that the pole is no longer under him.

7. Do this on both sides going sideways to both the right and left. Try completing this task with both direct pressure and then just air pressure.

Be sure to correct the horse right away if he goes forward. If the horse is uneasy or confused by going sideways over the pole, you can first ask for sideways with the pole in front of the horse.

Trouble Shooting:

It's common for horses to try and walk forward when doing sideways, or to step backward so that the pole is in front of them. This is why it's important to take one step at a time. Be sure to rest after each step for at least 10 to 20 seconds to allow your horse to think.

Starting the horse moving sideways with the pole in front of your horse can help him understand what is being asked. Once he's started taking sideways steps, you can move him forward over the pole and continue to ask for sideways.

Sideways Towards You

Cues: Sideways, yield the front end and yield the back end.

This is more difficult to teach, but very useful. For example, if you use a mounting block, you can simply use the sideways toward you cue and the horse will line up by the mounting block for you.

Steps to do sideways toward you:

1. Stand by a wall with at least 20 feet of room down the wall for you to work with. The idea for using the wall is that it will stop the horse from walking forward, and help him understand to move sideways. Remember that you will need the room behind you because you will be walking backwards (parallel to the wall) and the horse should be facing the wall walking sideways towards you. IMPORTANT: You should stand with your side very close to the wall. This is because you want to block the space between you and the wall; otherwise your horse may try to go through that space.

2. Stand against the wall holding your rope fairly short to the horse's head in the hand closest to the wall (this is one of the few times you may hold close to the rope halter, or under the chin of the horse), holding the stick in the hand closer to the hind end.

3. Start by holding your stick up and asking an ideal cue, which could be making a motion with the stick toward you. Keep the cue high, at chest level or higher, so that the cue makes sense to the horse and is distinguishable from other cues (this ideal cue needs to be different from your cue for come). Keeping the stick high and motioning toward you can mean sideways toward you, whereas keeping the stick low and motioning the stick at the horse's belly usually means sideways away from you. The horse will likely ignore this ideal cue the first few times, so you'll need to reinforce the cue by holding the stick over top of the horse with the tip of the stick touching his hip on the side furthest from you. (If you are standing on the left side of the horse, then your stick will be held over the horse, touching down on the right hip.) At first allow the string from your stick to hang over the hip and shake the string on the hip. If the horse does not move, then progress to tapping lightly and increase intensity tapping on the horse's hip until the horse's hip starts moving toward you.

Sideways Towards You

1. Lindsey lines Thetis up with the fence and starts with a light wiggle from the string as an ideal cue
2. Thetis moves her front-end but her hind-end is lagging
3. Lindsey gets Thetis to catch up her hind-end
4. Once Thetis has her hind-end square, she allows a break to reward her
5. Lindsey starts over with the ideal cue

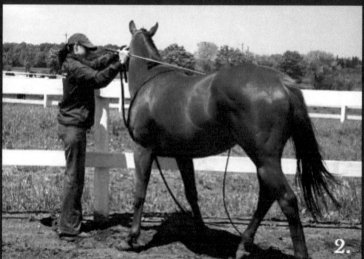

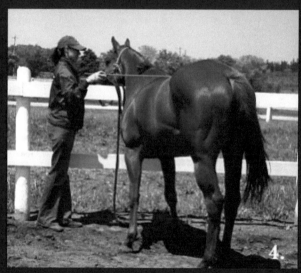

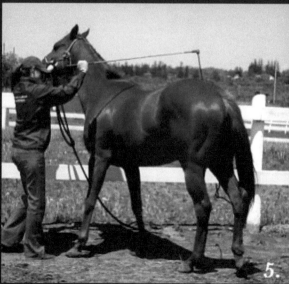

Sideways Towards You Over A Pole

1.

2.

3.

1. Lindsey starts by asking Ellie to halt with herself halfway over the raised pole.

2. Lindsey then motions for Ellie to walk toward her.

4.

3. Lindsey tries to keep Ellie straight by asking Ellie's hind end to catch up with her front end.

4. Lindsey moves Ellie one step at a time in order to keep Ellie's confidence up.

5.

5. Lindsey keeps Ellie going sideways until she is completely off the pole.

4. Once the horse moves the hind end towards you, stop, relax, and allow a minute of time for the horse to think.

5. Repeat steps 1 through 4 until your horse understands and you can move the hind end towards you with ease. Then you can progress to the next steps.

6. Ask the hind end for two steps toward you, then move the stick to the shoulder and ask the shoulder to move a step toward you (you will have to loosen up on the rope and step a couple of feet backward away from the horse to do this).

7. As soon as the horse takes a step with the front end toward, stop and pause for a minute.

8. Repeat steps 6 and 7. Once your horse understands this, you can then ask for sideways by moving the hind end a couple of steps, then moving the front end, and then try holding your stick over the middle of the horse's back and ask for a step towards you sideways. If the horse gets confused, then continue to ask the hind end to move a step, then the front end to move, and so on until the horse realizes that you want sideways. As soon as the horse moves sideways towards you, stop, rest, and allow the horse time to think—even if it's just one step!

Once your horse understands sideways, you can start to ask for more than just one step. Be sure to soften (go back to the ideal cue, or a much lower intensity) with every successful step, and after every couple of steps pause completely.

The idea is to be able to ask a horse to go sideways towards you from about 10 feet away using air pressure, or the pressure from the string dangling over the horse. Ideally you can get to the point where you can do about 20 feet or more of sideways towards you without going beyond the occasional light tap for increased intensity. Once you are able to ask for sideways towards you and the horse moves towards you without trying to go away from you first, you are ready to move away from the wall and try the game out in the open. If the horse walks forward then wiggle the rope to stop, or use the stick in front of the horse to stop. You can then advance this game to sideways towards you over a pole.

Trouble Shooting:

The horse may get confused with your ideal cue. Generally keeping the stick high and motioning towards you can mean sideways towards you, whereas keeping the stick low and motioning the stick at the horse's belly usually means sideways away from you. Keep this in mind when giving your ideal cue. You need to make sure that your cues are distinguishably different so the horse understands what each cue means.

A very common problem is that the horse will likely move away from you rather than towards you. This is because up until now, everything has been pushing the horse away from you, except for 'come.' If this happens, be sure to keep tapping at the same intensity that it took to get the horse

Playing at Liberty with Ellie
While Putting the Basic Cues to Work

1. Lindsey is playing follow me with Ellie. They are doing sideways in this picture. This is an excellent photo showing how focused Ellie is on Lindsey.

2. Lindsey is playing pole bending with Ellie, but is using buckets of flowers instead of weaving poles. This photo shows how Ellie is bending nicely around the buckets.

3. Lindsey sends Ellie over a small jump.

4. Lindsey is asking Ellie to come by patting her thigh. Ellie's alert and focused expression shows she is eager to join up with Lindsey.

1.

2.

3.

4.

Get Creative!

The goal is to stay out of a routine and in a conversation. You can use many different props and items.

moving in the first place. Keep the horse's nose pointed at the wall, and as soon as the horse takes one step with the hind end towards you, stop and rest to allow a reward and time for the horse to think.

Summary

There are many more games you can play with your horse. Some ideas include walking over bridges, through creeks, going up and down hills (or doing round abouts in an area with hills and ditches), walking into an exercise/yoga ball and pushing it around, leading the horse by looping the rope around the foot and lead by only putting pressure on the foot, walking over tarps, etc. The point is to get creative and to use props of all kinds, asking for patterns of all shapes and sizes. You might even turn your horse out, but instead of walking through the gate, try backing your horse through it. Try to make your time with your horse less of a routine and more of a conversation.

Think of new ways to get what you want. For example, if you want to warm your horse up before jumping, try leading your horse through a figure eight or barrel pattern while warming up, or introduce buckets, flowers, chairs, or other obstacles that you maneuver around while warming up. Get your horse thinking, test your communication, and keep your horse guessing and attentive to your cues. Remember the key is **stay out of a routine** and **stay in a conversation**!

Step 4: Let's Start Riding

Saddling

When it comes to saddling, the first thing you need your horse to learn is that all the tools are friendly. Take the time to allow the horse to sniff the saddle, pad, girth, and any other tack you may be introducing. You should be able to rub the tack all over the horse. If the horse resists or shows signs of being uncomfortable (tenses, pins ears, raises head, etc.) then keep rubbing in the uncomfortable area until the horse relaxes and is standing still. Once the horse is still you can stop completely and then back away or just move back to a spot you can rub that you know the horse enjoys. This is the principle of wait, retreat, and revisit.

If your horse is so scared of the saddle pad that you can't touch him with it, then get him to follow the pad by holding it in one hand, and the lead rope in the other hand, and just walk forward. After you walk forward long enough, the horse will become curious and initiate contact with the pad/tack, then you can rub the pad/ tack all over the horse.

Once your horse is comfortable with all of your tack, and you can rub your horse everywhere with your tack, you can proceed with the saddling steps.

Steps to saddling:

1.   Throw the saddle pad onto the horse's back. If he walks away, then wiggle the rope to stop, but leave the pad on the horse until he is still.

Saddling

1. & 2. Tossing the saddle pads on 3. Tossing the saddle on 4. The last weight bearing rib 5. Following the rib, checking the saddle is not too far back

6. Making sure the saddle is level 7. Tightening the girth 8. Tightening the girth again 9. Taking the horse for a short walk 10. Tightening the girth again with the horse's head up

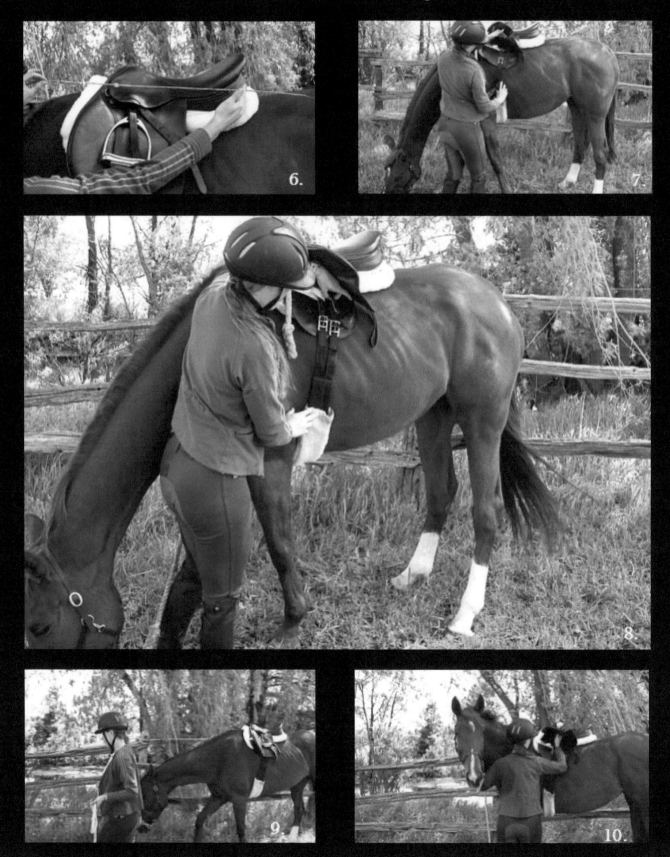

2.	Once the horse is standing still with the pad on his back, remove it and repeat step 1. You should be able to toss the pad onto the horse's back from both sides, three times in a row without the horse moving before you advance to the next step.

3.	Following the same procedure as with the saddle pad in steps 1 and 2, swing the saddle onto the horse's back. Try not to lift the saddle onto the horse, try swinging the saddle instead. Swinging the saddle is easier because you have momentum to get the saddle onto the horse's back. I recommend using a light saddle for easy tossing, and also a saddle that, if it falls to the ground or gets scuffed, you won't mind. When tossing the saddle onto the horse's back you want to be gentle and unthreatening, but at the same time you want to test the horse's tolerance and be as animated as you can be. The reason for this is because you want your horse to be able to tolerate a saddle thumping on his back, or if the saddle shifts awkwardly, you do not want the horse getting upset. By tossing the saddle up on the horse you teach him to be less sensitive to the process and it means if you accidentally fall onto the horse's back when mounting, he'll be less likely to spook. After all, if tossing a saddle on the horse's back scares him, do you really want to be up on his back? However, you don't want to test the horse every time—for the most part you want to be gentle, careful and considerate when saddling and mounting.

4.	Once you have the saddle on the horse's back you need to check the saddle fit. Even horses that have had the same saddle for years should have a quick saddle fit check because muscles can change in the horse and change the fit. Please see the section on saddle fit for more details.

5.	Tighten the girth, but only enough so that the saddle won't fall off or slip. If the horse walks forward while tightening, keep pressure pulling on the girth until the horse is standing still, then release the pressure on the girth.

6.	Walk the horse forward a few steps, then tighten the girth again.

7.	Send the horse on a round about at the walk, trot and canter if you have saddled less than a dozen times. If your horse has been saddled more than a dozen times then you can just do a round about at the walk, or at the walk and trot. If this is the horse's very first time being saddled, you may want to be in an enclosed round pen or small paddock/arena and take the horse off the halter/rope and send him on a round about at freedom. This way the horse is free to buck and run without the worry of being caught up in a rope. It is normal for a horse to buck, jump, and run for about 10 to 20 minutes if it's his first time being saddled, or the first time in a new type of saddle (first time with a western as opposed to an English, or the first time with an elastic girth, or the first time with an air pad).

8.	Tighten your girth again.

You do not need to toss the saddle pad/saddle up from both sides before every ride to make sure the horse is quiet, but during the initial training of a horse you want to test this task frequently to ensure safety. Once your horse is experienced with saddling, you should still always allow him to sniff/see the tack you are putting on his back and then proceed. If you are met with any form of resistance, such as a tail swish, pinned ears, walking forward, or stepping away, then you should take the saddle/pad off and re-saddle until the horse stands quietly. Ensure proper tack fit because many times an ill-fitting saddle will be the source of pinning ears or resistance.

Trouble Shooting:

Often the horse will walk forward when you toss the saddle or pad up onto his back. When this happens try to toss the pad/saddle more slowly onto the horse's back to ease tension. Once the pad is on the horse's back, leave the pad/saddle there until the horse is standing still, then you should remove the pad/saddle and repeat until you can toss the tack on the back without the horse walking away. This may take several tries, but will create a much more cooperative partner and trusting relationship.

Secondly, the horse may lose his patience and get bored. This means the horse will start to wander and may try to play with nearby objects. Try to be organized with your tack to prevent too much lag time. Have your tack all ready and in one spot. Practice tossing the saddle and pads up onto the fence before attempting to saddle the horse. Being coordinated will help you to be efficient with your time and appear like a more organized and worthy leader. You can also toss the pad up onto the horse, then play a different game or ask for a basic cue to try and keep your horse's focus, before trying the saddle. You can keep it simple, such as putting the pad on the horse, then asking the horse to yield the hind end a full circle each direction, then put the saddle on and tighten the girth, then yield the front end in a circle, etc. This will keep your horse focused and interested.

Playing a few games that involve a lot of movement such as round abouts, jumping, sideways, and pole bending are excellent games to play before saddling. This is because your horse will just have finished doing a lot of moving around and will likely want to stand still. If you can cause the horse to want to stand still, then he'll be more likely to stand quietly while saddling.

Mounting

Mounting is more than simply getting on a horse's back. Mounting a horse will give you the first indication of whether the horse is ready for you to be on his back or not. Paying attention to the horse during mounting is very important because it can let you know how the rest of your ride will go based on the reaction you get from mounting. Often riders mount their horses when the horse is not yet ready for a rider. This is evident when the horse fidgets, trying to avoid the mounting block, or when the horse is eager to walk off with you half mounted on his back. If you have mounted a horse that was not 100 percent willing and accepting of you, then you should get off and remount. You may need to play some games with your horse on the ground before mounting.

Playing games with your horse on the ground before mounting establishes good leadership and communication. It allows any 'bugs' in your communication, partnership, or leadership to be worked out before you even get in the saddle. A horse that listens attentively on the ground will likely listen equally as well once in the saddle. A horse that respects you on the ground will more likely respect you in the saddle.

Many horses that are termed 'hot' or really 'go-ey' are not really quick horses at all, but instead are just anxious about the riders being on their backs, and if proper mounting was done, then they would be a lot less quick and a lot easier to stop. This is because a horse's only two responses to fright are fight and flight. When the horse is being really quick and hard to stop, the horse is actually running from the rider. Having permission to be on the horse's back will give you the start to a better ride. Permission to be on the horse's back can be determined based on whether the horse stands still for you to mount, does not walk off until you ask, and stands still until you signal you are ready.

Sometimes horses will move around when you mount for other reasons, and these can be:

1) **Balance** - especially when mounting from the ground, the horse may feel the need to walk forward to support the weight being pulled to one side.

2) **Routine** - the horse may be familiar with a routine of the rider getting on and then walking off.

3) **Pain** - it may be too hard on the horse to mount from the ground so he may walk off.

4) **Too tight a girth** - sometimes when the girth/cinch is really tight, the horse feels the need to walk in order to breathe. This is because when at work, the horse breathes using the diaphragm and the movement from the shoulder helps this.

When assessing the quality of your mount and the readiness of your horse, it is important to consider the above four things that may be causing your horse to move about. If your horse is moving around due to one of the above four reasons, it is okay to continue riding. However, if the horse moves about out of lack of respect or readiness, then you should dismount and remount again until the horse is accepting of you. Dismounting and remounting will set you up for a much better ride.

Steps to an accepting and willing mount:

1. Start by standing facing the saddle at the side of the horse. You can mount from either side. Contrary to the many who believe you must always mount from the left, if you do not have a sword then there is no reason to mount from a particular side. Pick the side to mount from that best works for your situation. If you have a bad left knee then you may want to consider mounting on the right.

2. Hop up and down on the spot. This is to make sure the horse is accepting your stance; it will give a 'warning cue' to your horse that you are about to mount. If your horse is feeling anxious, you'll be able to tell by hopping rather than when you are half mounted on the horse and trying to swing your leg over! If the horse walks off, use one rein to keep the horse stopped. The horse may end up walking in a close circle around you— but it is important to only use one rein because this will prevent the trapping that we predators like to do and will allow you to stay in the same spot. Although you may end up turning in circles, your feet should stay on the same spot while hopping until the horse stands still. When the horse is still, you can relax and rub him somewhere that he enjoys.

3. Once you can hop on the spot for about five to six hops without your horse moving forward, then you can advance. Put your foot in the stirrup, hop three times and if your horse moves forward then keep hopping until the horse is still. This can take some balance to hop on one foot trying to keep the foot in the stirrup—if you cannot, then hop on two feet and put weight in the stirrup with a hand until the horse is fully stopped. When the horse is still, go back to rubbing a spot on the horse that you know he enjoys.

4. Once you can put weight in the stirrup and hop three times without the horse walking off, you can advance to the next step. Place your foot in the stirrup and stand up in the saddle but do not swing your leg over. If the horse is poorly balanced or has a bad back then be sure to fold yourself over the horse to help distribute your weight more evenly. If the horse walks off, then using one rein you can pull him to a stop/small circle, and when he's still you can dismount and rub him in a spot he enjoys.

5. Once you can do step 4 without the horse walking off, then you can advance. Now you can put your foot in the stirrup and fully mount. Your horse must stand still once you are mounting (he should not take any steps forward—although he may take a step to rebalance himself). This step can take several minutes, and is the most important part to be patient with. If the horse starts to walk off then stop him with one rein. Once stopped then dismount, rub the horse in a spot he enjoys and then mount again. Do this until you can mount without the horse walking off. You should be able to mount from both sides. You may have to use a stool if the horse is too tall for you, or if the horse has a bad back.

6. Once you have mounted, the first thing you should check is the lateral flexion of the horse. To do this, bend your horse's nose to his side so that his nose touches your leg. Simply turn his head—if he starts walking in circles just keep the pressure on the rein until he stops, then release the pressure when the horse is still. Doing this at the start of every ride, or at least once every other ride is a good idea. It bends your horse and increases his flexibility and range of motion. It also calms your horse because it's a position that releases endorphins, and it establishes that you will ask for things in the saddle that do not require moving the feet.

Mounting

1. Preparing to mount
2. & 3. Getting the horse used to a rider's weight
4. Fully mounted
5. Starting with lateral flexion

Sometimes this exercise can take up to an hour, but once you have been patient and carried this through, your ride will be much more enjoyable because the horse is accepting of you on his back.

To prevent the horse from learning a routine of mounting and then walking off, try to alternate what you do when you first get on. You can bend the horse's head from side to side, you can back him up, you can do a haunch turn, or go sideways. Be creative and always thinking so that your horse keeps thinking. Be careful not to be repetitive with your horse because if your horse falls into a routine then he can become quite upset when you break the routine—which may happen if you go to a show, go on vacation, have a friend ride your horse, etc.

Trouble Shooting:

Many handlers will get flustered when the horse keeps walking forward. When this happens you need to make sure you have one rein with contact on the horse's mouth/nose which will cause him to walk in a small circle around you until the horse decides it is better to just stand still. Once the horse is still, reward him by rubbing a favourite spot, or reward by doing nothing and just allowing him to stand for a minute. It is important to reward the horse for standing still; otherwise, the horse may think it is better to keep walking in order to not allow you to mount.

Patience is crucial. Once you start these logical steps, you need to commit to take the time to follow them through. If you run out of time and just end up hopping on anyways, you confirm in your horse's mind that you are still a predator at heart and not a partner. This is because you are putting your needs above your partnership needs. You would be giving your wants more priority than reducing your horse's anxiety. Remember that a good horse to mount is much more likely to be a good horse to ride. A bad mount will likely mean a ride with more testing from the horse, more attitude, and/or more anxiousness.

Your First Few Rides Together

Your first ride should be using a halter with a rope, or a rope hackamore, not a bridle with a bit. Riding with a bridle and bit when you have not established the finer communication with your horse is not the best idea. Putting a bit in the horse's mouth could put too much pressure on the horse and weaken the trust your horse has for you. This can make him less responsive because he can be too concerned with the pressure in his mouth. Think of using a bit as a way to refine what your horse already knows, or to advance skills your horse already knows. Therefore you start with something more basic like a hackamore.

Once you have mounted, you should start with lateral flexion. This means bending your horse's nose to the side so that his nose nearly touches your foot. This will teach your horse that riding

The First Ride

1. Mounted and allowing time to connect with the horse
2. Having patience to just sit still on the horse
3. Going into the walk
4. Taking the pace up to trot
5. Taking the pace up to canter

is not just about whoa and go; you teach your horse that you also just may ask him to bend his head from side to side. To do this, follow these simple steps:

1. Pick a side to bend to, either left or right.

2. Take the rein on the side you have chosen (left or right) and apply pressure pulling to your belly button to bend the horse's nose around. Increase pressure as needed to bend the horse's nose. If the horse is trying , do not increase pressure—only touch one rein and leave the other rein alone. Release the pressure once the horse is standing still with his head bent to the side (laterally flexed).

Trouble Shooting:

If he starts walking in circles just keep the pressure on the rein until he stops, then release the pressure when the horse is still.

If you are riding with just a rope and halter, bend your horse to one side, then toss the rope over the horse's head to check the other side and bend the other way.

Starting to Ride

Your first ride should be in an enclosed space, preferably a round pen with a diameter of 60 feet. Using a round pen will prevent your horse from getting 'stuck' in corners. If you don't have a round pen, use a fenced-in area of about 60 feet wide and long. You want enough space that the horse does not feel too much pressure from being in a cramped space, but you don't want so much space that the horse can get into a gallop or get excited. The largest enclosed area you should have for your first ride is an area of approximately 80 feet by 180 feet. Anything larger and you run the risk of your horse getting too excited and going faster than you may like.

It is recommended that you do NOT use a fenced-in area that has electric or wire fencing. Wooden fencing or solid walls are the best options.

Before you mount, you should practice lateral flexion on the ground. To do this, ask your horse to bend his head from side to side while you're on the ground. This makes it is easier for the horse to figure out what you're asking for when you're in the saddle and asking for lateral flexion. You should also check on the ground that you can toss the rope over the horse's head without the horse getting upset before doing so in the saddle.

Safety and relationship building are the number one priorities. Practicing what you can on the ground will help to prevent any surprises in the saddle. This means less confusion, which means you're less likely to experience dangerous behaviour such as bolting, bucking, or rearing.

Bending at the start of every ride, or at least once every couple of rides is a good habit. Lateral flexion bends your horse and increases his flexibility and range of motion, and as explained earlier, it calms the horse by being in a position that releases endorphins, and establishes that you will ask for things in the saddle that do not require moving the feet.

Steps for your first ride, in an enclosed space:

1. Ask for lateral flexion on both sides.

2. Once you have lateral flexion on both sides, ask your horse to move forward. Start with your ideal cue, and then increase the intensity. You may have to use the end of a rope, your stick, or a crop to assist your leg by tapping either side of the horse lightly behind your leg. As soon as the horse moves forward you need to release pressure, even if it is just a slow walk.

3. For your first ride, allow the horse to pick the direction and speed of the gait. All you need to do is control the gait (walk, trot or halt at this stage). This means your horse will get to choose if you do a slow or fast gait (so if you choose walk, then the horse can choose if it is a fast or slow walk—but as long as the horse is walking, you leave the horse alone). If this is the horse's first ride ever, you may want to just walk and trot around for about 10 to 15 minutes; then get off and play some more ground games.

4. If the horse has prior riding experience, then after approximately 20 minutes or so, you can start to get choosier with the speed in each gait—so you will ask for a slow, working, or forward walk/trot rather than just accepting any speed within the gait.

5. Once your horse is comfortable with you in the saddle at walk and trot, you can start to give direction. Start by playing 'follow the rail' and guide your horse over to the rail of your ring. When the horse drifts off, gently guide him back. Do this until the horse can do about two to three loops of the ring without coming off of the rail.

6. You are now ready to come off the rail and use a rope hackamore (if you weren't already). Now that you've established whoa and go, and the start to steering, it is time to further your steering. Two reins will help you with this. Work in a space of at least 60 feet in diameter. Start by allowing the horse to choose where to go. When the horse drifts (unless he's following a corner/curve of the ring), turn the horse around 90 to 180 degrees, so he's headed in a different direction. Keep doing this until the horse can consistently be pointed in a direction and will stay in a straight line until he has to turn (because of a wall/fence). The larger the ring, the better for this exercise. First play this game at the walk, then the trot, and then the canter. When playing this at the canter, you may need an open field if your arena is not very large. Always periodically double check that you can stop your horse by tensing your seat/ hips, leaning back slightly, lifting the reins, and then pulling back as needed, only releasing when the horse stops.

Trouble Shooting:

It is recommended that you have an experienced coach or trainer present when doing a first ride with a green horse, new horse, or if you are a beginner/novice rider. Many times the rider can make the horse stop, go faster, or turn just by tensing or shifting their body. Having a person watch your position can be of great assistance when trying to work out issues. Having a knowledgeable and experienced person watch you is never a bad idea!

When riding, be sure to keep equal weight in your stirrups and stay at the centre of gravity with your horse. If you are leaning too far forward it could make your horse go faster. If you lean too far back it could make your horse slow down or even stop. Leaning or putting more weight in one stirrup than the other can make your horse turn. Being careful to have still, quiet hands, paired with still and steady legs/feet, will help to make sure you do not interfere with your horse or send mixed signals. Tensing your hips, pinching the saddle with your knees, or not sitting on your seat (the cushy part of your bottom) can cause you to be tense in the saddle which can make your horse either anxious and quick, or reluctant to move forward.

Some tips for good position are to let your toe naturally turn out a little bit, keeping your ankle under your hip (or only slightly in front—you should not look like you are sitting in a chair with your legs out in front of you), hands relaxed and steady, a flat back, sitting straight up, and with your weight in your heels (your toes up and heels down). There are so many aspects of a rider's position to consider that I recommend you seek a coach or a friend who is knowledgeable and experienced to help.

Completing the Emergency Stop

Sometimes when riding, your horse may become spooked, or you may have to dismount quickly because of a broken piece of tack, injury, or to help someone else. Because you may not be able to use two reins, or you may not be able to stop a horse by simply pulling back, you should learn the emergency stop and teach it to your horse.

1. Pick a rein (either left or right); you will pick your side based on the canter lead your horse has, if applicable, and the environment you are in. For example, if you have a steep hill to your right, then you should probably turn your horse to the left. If your horse is on the right canter lead, then you should probably use the right rein.

2. Take the chosen rein (left or right) and pull to your belly button. Shorten the rein if needed in order to make contact with the horse's mouth. You can drop your opposite rein if needed. Be sure to sit up straight or slightly tilt back in order to maintain balance and not tip forward.

3. Pull the rein until the horse's nose is turned to your foot. Be sure to soften the rein immediately when the horse bends correctly and stops.

Lateral Flexion and Rein Aids
1. Bend Left 2. Bend Right 3. Left Open Rein
4. Right Indirect Rein 5. Left Direct Rein

1.

3.

4.

2.

5.

4. Then bend the horse a little a bit more and ask the horse to take a step with his hind end underneath him (see the photo on the right). This will disengage the horse, making him unable to dart forward without first fixing his feet. This means you will be using your left leg and left rein, or your right rein with your right leg. Remember you just want one step, so you shouldn't have to use too much leg.

5. You can now hold the horse in this position until it is safe to unbend him, or you can dismount on the side that the horse is bending (if the horse is bending to the left, then dismount on the left).

Using one rein to stop the horse takes away the trapped feeling that pulling back on two reins can sometimes give a horse. The trapped feeling can move horses towards being in a state of fight-or-flight (if they are not already), or it can make the frightened horse more frightened. In addition, bending the horse's neck to one side releases endorphins and has a calming effect on him. It's also easier to work a horse on one rein because he'll have a harder time resisting you with only one side of his neck muscles.

Direct Rein

To use a direct rein means that the pressure from the rein/bit is acting directly on one side of the horse's mouth. You pull directly back on the rein towards your hip (left rein to left hip or right rein to right hip), which will pull the horse's nose to that side. For example, if you pull on the left rein back toward your left hip, then the horse's nose will turn to the left and the horse will turn to the left if moving forward. This is the left rein acting directly on the bit.

Indirect Rein

Indirect rein pressure is using pressure on one side of the bit that causes the horse to move his hind end the opposite way. For example, if you pull on the left rein, but instead of pulling straight back, pull the rein upwards and toward your belly button (being careful not to cross the neck of the horse) then the rein will act indirectly on the horse. This means the left rein will cause the hind end of the horse to move to the right.

Indirect reins are also important when asking for bending and flexion. You can bend the horse in the direction you want by using the indirect rein. Using the indirect rein allows you to ask the horse to continue moving in a straight line. This is because you are able to bend the horse's head from side to side without turning or having to do a circle.

Indirect reins are useful when balancing a horse to keep his haunches in line with his body, when steering for balance (using both a direct rein and indirect rein together), or when asking for particular movements such as a forehand turn. Using both reins to turn can be very effective when in competition that requires precise turns. For example, using the left direct rein to pull the horse to the left and the right rein indirectly pulling towards your belly button to move the haunches to the left, will mean you are steering the body of the horse, not just the head, which will keep the horse straighter. **This can set you up nicely when competing in jumping sports or in equitation patterns.**

Open Rein

An open rein is similar to a direct rein except you move your hand away from your body and away from the neck line. Open reining can help clarify a cue for your horse, and directs the head, shoulders, and neck in the direction you are pulling. For example when you use an open rein on the left side, the horse should move his head, shoulders and neck to the left. **When using an open rein, think of taking your hand away from your body to point in the direction you want to go.**

Getting the Pokey Horse Going

A great example of using a crop to get a horse to go forward without inflicting pain or resorting to intimidation is as follows:

1. Start with your ideal cue and squeeze with both legs softy to ask the horse to move forward.

2. If the horse has not responded yet, then squeeze firmly.

3. If the horse still has not responded by moving forward, then kick lightly.

4. If the horse still has not responded by moving forward, then tap the crop/ swing the rope and tag your own leg to make a tapping noise.

5. If the horse still has not responded by moving forward then tap the crop/swing the rope behind your leg on the horse's side—hard enough that your horse knows you are communicating with him, but no harder than you would tap yourself. You want to be firm enough that your horse doesn't think you are just playing a desensitizing game (meaning you are trying to get your horse used to ignoring things bumping and hitting his sides).

6. If you have a rope you can swing it easily from side to side of your horse behind your leg—this is effortless on your part and usually causes a horse to go forward after a few tags on either side. If the horse still has not responded by moving forward, and you have a crop, then use the crop to poke the horse inside his ear. When poking the horse in the ear (just the entrance to the ear! You don't want to stick the crop deep into the ear risking damage to the horse) with the crop, as soon as the horse flinches, shakes, or moves forward, leave the horse alone. (If he

flinches stop!!! He doesn't have to move forward.) Start with your ideal cue again until you get the horse moving forward, and then until you get the desired pace/speed. While doing this, keep the contact with your leg, so that you are clear with your intent.

The idea behind this progression of cues is that you are trying to communicate to your horse that the right thing is comfortable and the wrong thing is uncomfortable and will get progressively more uncomfortable until he reacts. Be sure to **stop bugging your horse as soon as he moves forward**; this is critical to being successful at this task.

Also you must **progress through these steps within three seconds** each or the horse may think you are just playing a desensitizing game in which you are asking the horse to ignore you and stand quietly (which is a game we play with our horses when asking them to stand quietly while being bathed, clipped, dressed with blankets and many other things).

Being consistent in your approach is also very important because you want the horse to learn that you will always be fair by giving him the option to respond to the ideal cue, and lesser cues, but you also want him to know that you will always progress through the intensities in the same order—just like horses progress through their cues out in the paddock with their herd mates. Usually it only takes two to four tries, and your horse will figure out that if he doesn't move forward then you are just going to keep asking and then he will get poked in the ear. Because of the annoyance, the horse is motivated to recognize and respond to the ideal cue. Because you do not get rough with your horse, no dangerous behaviour such as bucking or bolting will be provoked.

Be careful not to abuse this task!!! If your horse is usually a little sluggish or pokey, and during a ride the horse offers to go forward, do not abuse it!!!! How many times have you seen a rider get a pokey horse into the canter, and then react by thinking, 'Great—now I can canter a couple of loops before the horse gets pokey again'? WRONG REACTION. When your horse offers something he doesn't usually do, do not abuse this. What this means is that if your pokey horse decides to offer canter easily, don't then canter several laps around the ring. Instead, only ask for one loop around the ring, or only 10 to 20 strides and then allow your horse to walk and have a break again. If you do this, you will notice your horse become more willing to offer more. This is because the horse will think you are fair.

To help illustrate this point, think about when your Mom used to ask you to clean your room, put away the dishes, do your homework for the day, or some other task. Now imagine if after a day at school you came home and did all the things your Mom usually asked because you wanted to please her... except when she got home she simply responded by saying, 'Great, now you can also clean my bedroom, make my bed, and do the laundry.' How likely are you to offer to do all your chores the next day? Or even the next month? Or even ever? The same thing goes for horses. You are a leader, but also like a responsible parent. You have to provide a focus, a task, and see that the task gets accomplished in a way that is fair, respectful, and clearly communicated in order to have a successful partnership with your horse.

Be grateful for what your horse offers. When working with a horse that is generally pokey, be grateful when he is really responsive. This means that if this pokey horses offers canter when you only asked for trot, allow him to take a couple strides of canter before bringing him down to trot. This way you are being part of a partnership that acknowledges efforts from your partner (the horse) and allows your partner to have input. This means your horse will be more likely to work for you in future tasks. Likewise if you had a generally quick horse, when that horse offered to be really slow, you would allow him to be slow for a little bit before picking up the pace. This is assuming of course that you do not want a really pokey or a really go-ey horse.

Bridling and Bits

Contrary to common belief, the hackamore, or riding with a rope and halter is the initial tool you should use for riding your horse, not a bridle with a bit. This is because the rope and halter are the most basic in communication and you can steer your horse and ask for go and stop with these tools. With the rope hackamore you can ask clearly for turns and stopping and there is no need for a bit. A bit provides advanced communication and is used to teach cues that require subtleties that can better be felt with a bit. Teaching advanced cues using a bit can make it easier to then teach the cues without a bit later.

Introducing a Bit

The first couple of times you ride with a bit, ride with both the bridle/bit and the hackamore. Bridle the horse over top of the hackamore, and ride using just the hackamore reins. Allow the bridle just to be present, but not actively used. This will allow the horse time to get used to the bit in his mouth.

You should not use a noseband. Nosebands prevent a horse from communicating to you when there is too much pressure in his mouth. You should start with a very soft and simple bit like a snaffle or French link. I prefer French links because when you pull back on a snaffle, the bit bends with a point digging into the top of the horse's mouth which is harsher than a French link, which has a flat piece across the tongue.

You are ready to pick up both sets of reins (the hackamore and the bridle reins) and ride using both sets once you have accomplished these three things: 1) Your horse can be bridled with a bit, 2) you have ridden a couple of times with the bridle/bit on in combination with the hackamore, using only the hackamore reins, and 3) the horse has completed the rides without chomping on the bit. Over the course of a couple of rides, start to use the bridle reins more than the hackamore reins.

After a few rides you should be able to ride the horse with just the bridle reins, but still have the hackamore on for back up in case the horse is experiencing too much pressure in the mouth (you will know this because the horse will open its mouth if there is too much pressure in the mouth). Once you have ridden a few times using the bridle reins only, without the horse fighting the bit at all, you are ready to ride with just the bridle and bit.

Having the bit in the horse's mouth will allow you to have clearer communication when using a direct, open, and indirect rein. Teaching your horse these cues, and asking for bending, flexion and other more advanced movements is easier when using the bit. Riders who are more advanced may use a bit to help the horse understand the cues given by the rider's body so that eventually he can be ridden with no bridle at all.

Beginners and novices should use the most appropriate tool when riding. For example, there is no reason for a beginner to ride with a bridle that has double reins and Pelham bit. Unless the rider understands the advanced workings of a Pelham and double reins then it is unnecessary. If the reason for a bit with a chain under the chin is to give more control, then the rider should do more work on the ground to establish trust and respect with the horse.

Understand that a 'hot' horse or a really forward horse is often running from the rider because he is anxious. Another reason for a 'hot' horse can be due to a lack of turn out and/or play with other horses, or from being fed foods that are too rich.

Remember that the horse's natural response to fear is fight-or-flight. Often when a horse appears 'hot' the horse is really just trying to take flight from the rider. Taking the fear away from the horse by establishing a trusting and respectful relationship will also take away the 'hot' behaviour if this is the cause. If the cause of the 'hot' behaviour is because the horse is fresh from lack of turn out or lack of social interaction (playing with other horses, toys/objects, and dominance play) then you should consider allowing your horse to free lunge (letting your horse run around loose in an arena), giving your horse adequate turnout, and giving your horse a playmate or two if he doesn't have one already.

Back Up

Before you start to back up you need to decide what your ideal cue will be, and also make sure your horse backs easily on the ground. Some types of ideal cues when mounted may be:

1) Holding your legs in front of the horse's shoulder and flapping gently.

1) Gently and subtly swinging your leg in a backward motion against the side of the horse.

2) Tilting backward.

3) Picking up the rein and slightly pulling back.

4) A combination of the above.

Steps to backing up:

1. Start with your ideal cue. If the horse does not move then increase the intensity and clarify the response by tilting backward, stopping any forward motion by pulling back, and adding energy

by putting pressure on the horse's side from your toe to your heel. When you ask a horse to go forward you usually start with your heel and then close your toe, so when backing up, first put pressure with your toe and then roll your foot/calf against the horse so that your heel makes contact last with the horse. This makes a backward motion to the horse.

2. At first just ask for one step at a time. Then, as the horse begins to understand, you can soften your cue after the first step (go back to the ideal cue, or pause for a moment if the horse responded to the ideal cue) and then ask for another step and so forth until you have the number of steps you want.

The Sit Trot

The sit trot is avoided by many because it can be uncomfortable, but with these helpful tips you will find it easier. Practice sit trot at a slow pace and with no stirrups to help you get into the right position.

Steps to a good sit trot:

1. To start, over exaggerate the position by extending your legs out in front of you, which will roll your seat bones underneath you and tilt your hips (a pelvic tilt). **This means you should be sitting on the cushy part of your bottom.**

2. Take one hand and place your thumb on the top of the back of your saddle. Try to roll your upper seat/lower back to your thumb (this will over exaggerate the pelvic tilt). This is hardest in a close contact saddle because the back of the saddle is not very high, so use your discretion about how much to roll your hips.

3. Stay in this position during the trot. You will find that you can sit much easier when on the 'cushy' part of your bottom (not your tailbone) and roll your seat underneath you (doing the pelvic tilt).

4. When you take your stirrups back, still roll your seat and do the pelvic tilt, and extend your legs out in front of you if this helps you get into position.

Gaiting

Gaited horses are some of the most majestic of breeds, with their flowing movement and comfortable gaits. Gaited horses are renowned for their ability as pleasure horses and suitability to those with bad backs and stiff joints. Gaited horses can provide a comfortable ride at a reasonable speed with their unique foot fall patterns.

Gaiting a horse can be quite confusing. First you need to understand what gaiting means. Gaiting is a four-beated gait, the same as a walk, except it is roughly the same speed as a trot. Four beated means that each of the four feet of the horse land at a different time—each foot lands independently of one another. When you compare this to a trot, you will see that the horse moves his legs in pairs and two feet land together at the same time.

For different breeds, gaiting is coined with different terms to distinguish the breed. Different examples are tolting, racking, and fox trotting, which are specific to certain breeds of horses but are ultimately a similar comfortable gait.

Only certain breeds of horses have the ability to gait. These breeds include Kentucky Mountain Horses, Rocky Mountain Horses, Icelandic Horses, Mustangs, Fox Trotters, Paso Finos, and more. I have had the pleasure of working with gaited breeds at Pleasure Valley. Pleasure Valley is home to Mustangs, Tennessee Walking horses, Kentucky Mountain horses, and a Paso Fino.

Standardbreds may commonly pace, which is a speed similar to a trot, and is also two beated like a trot, except the legs on each side of the horse move together rather than in diagonal pairs (this means the legs move in lateral pairs). Pacing horses will move both left legs forward and then land together, and then the right side move and land together. A pace is generally smoother than a trot, and gaiting is usually even smoother, making it the smoothest movement a horse can do—even better than canter!

A horse cannot jump while pacing or gaiting, the horse must be walking, trotting or cantering in order to jump—this is why when out on a trail and gaiting, a horse will fall out of gait and switch to trot in order to go over a log.

All gaited horses also have the ability to trot and pace. Not all trotting horses have the ability to pace and trot. A trotting Thoroughbred or Quarter Horse does not have the ability to learn to gait, but a gaiting Mountain Horse can learn to trot. This is because gaiting is a genetically given trait that gives the horse another foot fall pattern to follow, but the structure of the horse is not different at all. Therefore the conformation of a gaited horse is the same as that of a trotting horse, although some breeds may have preferences for slight differences. The gaiting difference is that the gaiting horse is genetically programmed to know how to move his feet in such a pattern that allows him to gait.

Gaited horses can be excellent choices for people with bad backs, or riders who enjoy a smooth ride. However, gaited horses are not able to compete in many events that require a trot. There are certain breed specific shows, and some types of shows allow gaiting, and generally have classes specific to gaited horses. If you are interested in competing with a gaited horse, you need to look into the competitions available in your area.

Some horses are naturally gaited, which means that even in the paddock they walk, gait or canter, but never trot or pace; these horses are the best to learn to gait on because there are few worries of the horse falling out of the gait into a pace or trot. Other horses switch in and out of gaiting/trotting/pacing and require the rider to balance them in a way that helps them pick the

Gaiting, Pacing, and Trotting

1. Mojo is trotting, which means his legs are moving in diagonal pairs

2. & 3. Hawk is pacing, which means his legs are moving in lateral pairs (both left legs together and both right legs together)

4. & 5. Phantom is gaiting, which means each hoof lands independently of one another

1.

2.

3.

4.

5.

right foot fall pattern that the rider wants. Usually a horse will either be more inclined to trot or pace and there are different exercises for both.

Gaiting is a four-beated gait that is considered to be in-between pacing and trotting, which are both two-beated gaits. If a horse is inclined to trot and you want him to gait, then you should try to do exercises that move the horse toward being a pacer. If the horse paces, then you want to do exercises that will push him towards a trot.

Going up hill will encourage a horse to trot, and going downhill is more likely to put a horse into a pace. Going over an obstacle will always put the horse into trot (unless at a speed where he can walk or canter).

Teaching a horse to gait is an advanced skill and requires a feel developed from riding gaited and trotting horses to learn the different balance for each gait. You have to move your body in a way that mimics the movement of a gait. You need to recognize when you are out of gait so you can quickly correct the horse. The horse will ride in whatever foot fall pattern he does most often, which is why it is important to correct a horse right away if he falls out of gait (unless you do not care for the gait). It is easier for a horse to gait if his head is held up higher than wither level and when movement of the head is allowed—a gaiting horse will usually have a slight head bob.

When asking a horse to gait, do it from a walk because walking is a four-beated foot fall pattern, rather than trying to ask for a gait while in a pace or trot. This is because trotting and pacing are two-beated foot fall patterns. If your horse begins to pace or trot, come down to a walk, reorganize, and ask again.

Try having your horse follow a gaited horse. If your horse constantly rides with trotting horses, he may learn the trot pattern and be less inclined to gait. Likewise, if your horse is following other gaited horses, he may pick up the gait on his own.

If you are having gaiting issues I recommend you contact a professional near you with experience training gaited horses.

Bending and Collecting

Bending means the horse bends from side to side, also termed lateral flexion. If your horse is bending the correct way, you should be able to see the inside corner of his eye on the side you are bending (if you are circling to the left or riding on the left rein, you should be able to see the left eye). The bend should carry all the way down the horse's body so that there is slight bend through the ribs as well. Feeling for a complete bend is more of an intermediate skill and assistance from a knowledgeable person is recommended.

Collecting is the organization of the horse into shorter strides, a rounded top line, and bearing more weight on the haunches. Generally the horse carries more weight on the forehand, and the

Bending and Collecting

1. Correct bend and collection

2. Slightly above the bit

3. Slightly behind the bit

4. Above the bit at the trot

haunches are primarily used to propel the horse forward. When collected, the horse carries more weight on the hind end, which puts him in a position of power and better able to do jumping, dressage, and other advanced movements.

A rounded top line means the spine of the horse is rounded. If the horse is hollow it will look like the horse's head is up, his nose sticking up and out, and the hind end will not be tucked under and instead may appear to be dragging behind. A rounded top line will have an arch to the horse's neck, nose vertical to the ground (tucked in), and the hind end rounded under, bearing more weight.

Think of collection as being energy that is upward, whereas usually energy comes in the form of forward energy. Forward energy is energy that propels the horse forward. To collect a horse and get upward energy, energy from the rider's leg that would normally move the horse forward is instead captured in the hand, blocking the forward motion, which brings the energy upward creating a rounded and powerful stance. Be careful not to over flex your horse (over collect) to the point where his head is tucked into his chest—it makes it more difficult to perform movements and is also a very unnatural position.

Bending is correct balance in the way in which the horse is moving. A horse can have the correct bend but not be collected. A horse can be collected but not be on the right bend. A horse should be bending in the direction you are going (if you are riding on the right rein, then you should have the horse bending to the right). When bending a horse, you have to be careful not to over bend. This means that the horse bends the head and neck too much, so that the shoulders drift and makes turning more difficult. The shoulders should stay straight with just a slight bend in the neck/head toward the direction you are going, and a bend through the rib cage around your leg.

When learning bending and collection it is important that you don't over bend or over flex your horse. When teaching bending and collecting to your horse, remember that this type of work requires more energy and your horse will need more rest periods or shorter work outs until the horse is fit enough.

To help with bending you can practice circles in varying sizes, changes of direction, and riding patterns like serpentines and figure eights. To help with collection, start on a circle. Be steady with the outside balancing rein, using the leg with the hand to support the horse. Because collection is capturing energy, the amount of leg you use will depend on the horse. Slow horses require more leg to create energy, whereas a horse more sensitive to the 'go' button would need less leg. When your horse is collected the way you want him to be, leave him alone! Remember that collection is turning forward energy into upward energy, so if there is no energy to collect, then you need to create energy by adding your leg to the horse.

When working on bending and collecting, start by shortening and lengthening the stride on the circles and going straight. Work on turns and circles, making sure to have the correct bend. Be sure

1. Cantering on the right lead, the leading right front hoof has not yet left the ground
2. Cantering when the leading right hoof is the first to extend forward of the four legs
3. The walk (each hoof lands independently of one another)
4. The trot (the hooves land in pairs)
5. Cantering on the left lead (the leading left hoof and the right hind hoof land individually, but the right front and left hind hooves are paired and land together)

Canter Leads and Different Gaits

3.

1.

4.

2.

5.

to use a soft bit that is comfortable for your horse. Too much pressure in the mouth will cause the horse to try to avoid the bit.

Seek experienced guidance, because bending and collecting are advanced skills that are best learned with a helpful eye watching you as every horse is different. In general, remember that you want the right thing to be comfortable and the wrong thing to be uncomfortable. This means that when the horse is responding correctly, you need to be still and reward the horse by leaving him alone with your hand and leg. This does not mean that you let your reins go slack and stop supporting your horse. It means that you keep your legs and hands still and allow the horse to continue balancing. As soon as the horse moves out of the bend/collection you want, you need to start asking again right away. This will help to reinforce that the wrong thing is uncomfortable, and will help the horse recognize what is desired and what is not. Failing to correct the horse right away will confuse the horse as to whether you even know what you're asking for.

Canter Leads and Flying Lead Changes

Flying lead changes are a skill performed at the canter. When horses canter they lead with one of their front legs. A horse on the left lead will extend the left legs further than the right. When teaching leads, it can be helpful to use coloured wraps or bandages on the horse's legs. For example if you put a yellow wrap on the horse's front left leg, it is easier to refer to it as the yellow leg for expediency.

A flying lead change is when the horse stays in the canter rhythm and switches from leading with one set of legs to the other. This means a horse can switch from the left canter lead to the right or vice versa. It is usually easier to ask a horse to switch canter leads by breaking out of canter and going into trot, than to ask for the other canter lead while still in canter. Horses will usually pick up the lead according to the direction they are going. For example, if you ask for canter coming out of a corner of the ring where you are turning left, then the horse is likely to get the left lead. If you are asking for canter in a round pen while following the rail of the round pen to the right, you are likely to get the right lead.

In addition to being able to see a wrong lead, if you are riding you should be able to feel it. A wrong canter lead while riding will usually feel quite awkward when on a circle or turning a corner. This is because the horse is leading its body to the wrong side and will try to lean and bend awkwardly to try and compensate. Generally, even beginner riders can feel a wrong lead because of how 'off' it feels.

A horse can learn the correct canter leads through repetition with the rider perfecting the cue for the right and left leads. If you are just a pleasure rider who mostly trail rides, then canter leads may be unimportant to you unless you plan to canter around tight turns that may require more balance. Correct canter leads are most important for ring work that involves turns, circles, and jumping, all of which require proper balance. A horse making a left turn on the right lead will be unbalanced in the turn and coming to a jump out of an imbalanced turn will affect the quality of the jump or the next task ahead.

Counter cantering is essentially cantering on the wrong lead. This means that if you are turning to the right, the horse would be cantering on the left lead. Counter canter is considered an upper level dressage move or an upper level equitation task. This means you could be asked for counter canter during competition when you get above basic levels. You should only ask for counter canter once your horse has a solid understanding of the cues for right and left leads so that you do not confuse your horse.

Always ensure correct saddle and tack fit, and rule out any underlying problems that could affect your horse not getting correct leads, such as conformational problems, muscle knots, or structural strains that may require chiropractic, massage, or veterinarian treatment.

In order to teach flying lead changes, your horse must first understand the correct leads. Practice by circling in each direction on the correct lead. If your horse picks up the wrong lead, come back to trot in a corner/on a circle, so you can correct the lead within three to five steps of trot as you are coming out of a corner to make the correct lead more clear to your horse. You want to bring the horse to trot for only three to five steps so that he understands you are making a correction. If you trot for too long after a wrong lead, the horse will not associate the two events together and will just think you are now trotting.

Before you correct a wrong lead, you can canter around one corner, or one circle to show the horse how uncomfortable cantering on the wrong lead can be. After all, you want the correct lead to be comfortable and the wrong lead to be uncomfortable in order to show the horse what you are asking for. When the horse gets the correct lead, you should reward the horse with your voice and a friendly rub, and then only do a few strides before allowing a break. The last thing you want your horse thinking is, 'Oh shoot, when I gave my rider that canter lead I had to do five laps around the ring; I definitely won't do that canter lead again!' To prevent your horse from thinking that way, reward him by only doing a few strides, then allow walking for a little bit, then ask for canter again. Slowly increase the number of canter strides or loops in the ring you do to build your horse's stamina.

Flying lead changes are a natural movement that horses will often do in the paddock when at play. Horses by nature want to be balanced because being balanced will mean they're at less risk for falling or tripping. Being careful to stay balanced is important to a prey animal because tripping or falling could mean a predator could catch them. Therefore a horse is already motivated from birth to learn flying lead changes. Foals can be seen doing flying lead changes days after birth when frolicking about.

Flying lead changes can be important for several disciplines. For many cases, flying lead changes allow you to correct a wrong lead without breaking stride into a trot, which means no pace or speed is lost. Flying lead changes allow you to correct a wrong lead more easily and quickly which is helpful when speed is a factor. Being on the correct lead is important for turning, balancing, and advanced communication with your horse. A horse capable of doing flying lead changes can have a faster time in speed events, or a more solid and safe round when jumping. Sometimes flying lead changes can be a required task in competition such as reining and dressage. In some competitions doing a simple change (breaking to trot and then asking for canter again) instead of a flying lead change can give you a deduction in your score such as in a hunter over fences class.

Steps to asking for flying lead changes

1. Start by teaching your horse a pattern of a figure eight. Do this by riding a figure eight 4 to 5 times at the trot so the horse learns the pattern and can anticipate the turns. (A figure eight is riding a 20m circle to the right and then a 20m circle to the left—so if viewed from above, it would look as if you were drawing the number 8. You can ride figure eights with larger or smaller circles depending on your needs and purpose).

Example of a Figure 8 Pattern:

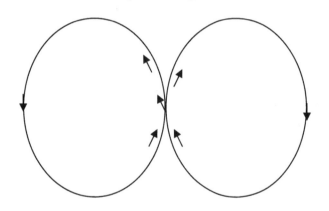

2. Pick up your canter and start to canter your figure eight. Your horse will likely not switch his lead when he changes direction, but allow him to continue cantering around the first bend of the circle so he can feel how awkward a turn is on the wrong lead. Then break to walk (not trot), and pick up the canter again. Do several of these figure eights so that you change directions about five times each way. Breaking to walk rather than trot makes the simple change more inconvenient and more uncomfortable than the flying lead change. Walk to canter transitions are difficult and require a lot of energy, so your horse will be more motivated to find the desired response if you walk instead of trot. Only let the horse walk a step or two before asking for the correct lead; that way the horse knows you are making a correction versus just giving him a walking break. However, do remember to allow walk breaks throughout your workout!

3. Do step 1 and 2 every couple of rides or every ride at least four to five times. Once you have done this, the horse should start to anticipate the change in direction and change the lead. The horse may end up doing a flying lead change without the rider giving any cue at all—if this happens, reward right away by rubbing and allowing the horse to walk.

4. After your horse understands the pattern and understands that you will change his lead, ask him to keep cantering through the circle and apply your ideal cue for the lead

change. This should be very subtle because any big shift in your weight will actually prevent the horse from doing a flying lead change. A slight tap with your outside leg, sitting and bring your inside hip forward, etc. are all subtle cues that will not threaten your horse's balance. Any big cues that alter your weight distribution can threaten his balance, which means the horse will just stay on the wrong lead. As soon as your horse gives you the flying change, reward by rubbing and then allow a walk break before you ask for another change. If you get too greedy and try to ask for several in a row, then your horse may stop doing them, because if you do not reward him he may think he's doing something wrong. After all, the correct response shouldn't lead to more work, right?

5. If your horse does not offer the flying lead change, then you can set up a pole in the middle of the ring, and also on the corners of the ring. Use the pole as a small jump, which will get the horse to pick up his legs a little more and help him to do the change. Use the pole in the centre of the ring because this is the desired place of the change of lead, and use a pole on the corner of the ring as a 'back up' in case the horse did not change over the first pole. Remember to reward as soon as your horse does the change of lead, and allow a walk break before you ask for another change.

Trouble Shooting:

The horse may change only the front or back end of the canter lead, instead of both the front and back legs. When a horse does this, it is termed cross cantering. When this happens, keep the canter and stay in a circle, bringing the horse to a slow, balanced canter. The horse should then be able to swap the rest of the lead. If not, then take the horse over a pole at the canter and he should swap. If the horse is still on the wrong lead then do a simple change (break to trot, then ask for canter again).

Placing poles in the corners of your ring will help the horse get the change (rather than putting them only in the centre of the ring which is often done). You place the pole so that when you cross the diagonal of the ring, the horse then steps over the pole in the corner which encourages the flying change.

Be sure you are being fair when you ask for a flying change. Your horse must be in good physical form to perform flying lead changes, so if you only ride your horse once a week or every other week, it may not be fair to be asking for flying lead changes.

Be careful not to twist your body, and to not allow your horse to twist. Big changes in balance may make your horse lack the confidence to try a flying lead change.

You can also practice flying leads during freedom work by asking for the canter in one direction and then directing the horse across the ring while still at the canter. If your horse is not fit enough to do a flying lead change during freedom work, then chances are it will be extremely difficult for him to do them under saddle. This is because lead changes take balance. Some horses are more naturally well balanced than others. Horses with long backs, or that are steep in their hind end may have particular trouble with this task.

Maintaining balance and straightness are keys to completing the flying lead change. Over bending or over flexing your horse can throw off his balance and make it impossible for him to swap the lead. Keeping the horse in the appropriate pace is also important so that your horse doesn't try to run and use speed to do the lead change. If your horse is trying to use speed to do the lead change, it is probably because he is out of shape or nervous about the lead. Make sure you are quiet with your body (hands and legs are still, no major shifts in your weight, no leaning to one side, etc.). If you move around too much, you could be making your horse nervous about the lead change. Condition your horse to make sure he is fit, by working him regularly (three to five times per week, for 30 minutes or more). You can help to condition a horse by practicing circles and riding up and down hills. Trotting up and down hills is an excellent way to get your horse in shape. You can also back your horse up hills to develop strong haunches (start with a few steps).

Transitions

Transitions are changes in gait and include: backwards, halt, walk, trot, jog, extended trot, lope, canter and extended canter. When first practicing with a horse, focus on just halt, walk, and trot. Concentrating on these transitions with an unfit horse or a novice rider can help build rhythm, balance and fitness before advancing to canter. You always should ask for transitions and changes of pace that are considerate of the rider and horse level so that you can always have success. Once you have backwards, walk, trot and canter gaits, you can further your horse's training to include jog/collected trot, lope/collected canter, extended trot, and extended canter.

Extension means bigger strides and does not mean faster; collection means a shorter step, not slower. Being able to control your horse's step within a gait gives you better control which helps you to balance, find a take off spot to a jump, ride in rugged terrain, and to demonstrate better leadership and communication which can lead to further advanced skills.

Steps to flawless transitions:

1. First establish the cues. For walk I use a gentle short squeeze with both legs and for trot I use a gentle longer squeeze. For canter I use both legs with more pressure coming from one leg (more pressure with my left leg signals a right canter lead to my horse, and more pressure with my left leg signals a right canter lead). You can pick whatever ideal cue is best for you, but make sure that it will make sense to your horse, based on pressure and position.

2. Start by asking for transitions between one gait (halt to walk, canter to trot, halt to backwards, etc. but not walk to canter, or halt to canter). Ask with your ideal cue and increase intensities. For halt I generally tense my hips and lean back slightly; you want to create the feeling of 'I've quit riding forward' which should signal the horse to completely halt. You can even bring your legs slightly away from the horse to signal that you've 'quit.'

For canter to trot I switch my position to a post, or my seated position to the movement felt at a sit trot. For slowing to a walk I move my body to the motion felt at walk. To slow down, if my horse does not first respond to my body, I use a half halt—pull back on both reins briefly, soften, and repeat until the horse responds. You cannot continually pull on both reins or you take on a trapping-like behaviour, which can make the horse anxious and will not slow him down. Reinforce your ideal cue if the horse does not respond. When asking a horse to move up a gait (from walk to trot or from trot to canter) then you may use a stick/crop/rope and tap your own leg to make a tagging sign as a warning, and then advance to tagging the horse. For slowing this may require a firmer half halt and tilting farther back.

3.   Be sure to stop asking as soon as the horse gets the gait you desire—even if it isn't the pace you want. As your relationship grows and you have understanding, you can progress to choose the pace within a gait and ask for a more extended canter or collected canter, etc.

4.   Once you have established consistency, balance and accuracy when moving between one level of transition, you can then move between two levels (walk to canter, or halt to trot) and once those transitions are consistent, balanced, and accurate, you can then move between three levels of gait (halt to canter, backwards to trot).

The focus is on clear communication by means of a consistent, unique cue, and a crisp transition. For instance, if asking for trot from the walk, you want the horse to move right into a trot without a period of fast walking first.

Trouble Shooting:

You should only be working on crisp transitions once your horse understands more leg means go, and more rein means whoa. You ride a horse with your whole body—when you slow your horse it shouldn't just be with your reins, your body position is important too. Having a knowledgeable person available to watch and help is very beneficial because often riders will have positional errors that are creating problems. If these concepts are not understood then your horse could get worried or discouraged. Horses learn the basics of whoa and go by practicing halt, walk and trot transitions with time spent in each gait to reaffirm in the horse's mind that he is in the right gait.

Usually horses will be either easier to slow and whoa, or easier to go and get moving. The objective is to try and help horses to be equally good at both slowing and going. To do this you have to make sure that you don't make a sensitive button more sensitive, nor make a dull button duller. This means that if a horse is already eager to go you shouldn't be practicing walk/canter transitions or halt/trot transitions because you are just making the horse more sensitive to go. Instead you should be working on downward transitions through two gaits such as trot to halt or canter to walk. The upward transitions should remain through one level such as walk to trot or trot to canter. This will help to make the horse less sensitive to go, and more responsive to slowing cues.

If your horse is hard to get going, you want to practice upward transitions and then reward right away by letting the horse walk. When horses realize that you won't use up all their energy if they offer it to you, then they'll be more likely to offer it again. Meaning that if the horse offers you canter right away, and you respond by letting the horse walk, then he's more likely to offer canter right away the next time.

Forehand Turns

Forehand turns are usually easier to do than haunch turns, so it is a good idea to teach the forehand turn before the haunch turn to keep your horse's (and your) confidence up.

Before asking in the saddle for a forehand turn, be sure your horse can perform one on the ground. Refer to the forehand turn section under Basic Cues for further instruction on this task. Once you are able to do a full circle of a forehand turn on the ground, you are ready to try in the saddle.

For this example we are doing a forehand turn to the right, meaning the horse's hindquarters will move to the left, but the horse's head will be turning to the right. The horse should pivot on the right front foot.

Steps to completing a forehand turn in the saddle:

1. Place your right leg just slightly behind the normal leg position. Then ask with your ideal cue. If the horse does not respond, add pressure with your right leg, then to increase the cue, add the right rein to turn the horse's head to the right. Only use the left rein as brakes in case the horse starts to walk forward (in combination with the right rein).

2. With each step the horse takes in the correct direction, you should soften before you ask for another step.

This means you will be using the lateral aids. Lateral aids refers to the leg and rein on the same side as your primary aids (right leg and right rein in the above example) using the opposite rein as brakes (the left rein in the above example).

Being able to yield your horse's hindquarters helps to make advanced skills such as haunches in, leg yielding, and maintaining straightness within gaits easier because you know how to control the legs of your horse. This means that you can steer the horse's body, not just the head.

Trouble Shooting:

Sometimes riders can get active with their hands. This means too much pressure in the mouth. Usually this is also paired with not enough action with the leg. The rider should start with leg and then add rein as needed. This is often expressed by the horse in one of two ways: 1) opening the mouth while raising his head trying to avoid the bit or 2) backing up. When you experience these

Forehand Turn (move the haunches)

1. Andrea asks Lora for the forehand turn by using her right rein to turn Lora's nose to the right, and her right leg to push Lora's hind end to the left.

2. Andrea is doing a good job at keeping Lora's front right hoof planted on the ground, while asking her hind end to swing to the left. Notice the hind legs crossing over.

3. Lora is stepping to the side nicely to complete the forehand turn. Andrea has started tilting a little bit forward and demonstrates how leaning forward shifts your balance, which makes it more difficult for Lora to do the pivot turn. Notice how Lora is now over bent to the right.

4. Andrea is sitting up taller again, which shows you how the shift in balance has allowed Lora to get a bit straighter. Andrea is showing a common mistake riders make by putting her right hand quite low, so the rein is not acting as an indirect rein (which would be going to her belly button). This picture also shows how the hind end has been turning because of the tracks created in the sand; Andrea has managed to complete an accurate turn.

problems, keep pressure in the mouth but use less; then add more leg as needed. Be patient and wait for the correct response, then reward by simply sitting and taking a moment to relax.

Occasionally the horse can become confused because of the rider's position. Position your body to encourage the movement you want i.e. shift your weight in the direction you want to go. This will help make the objective clearer to the horse. If you sit perfectly square in the saddle with no difference in your weight or balance, then the horse can get confused thinking, 'Isn't this how they sit when we are going straight?' Make things easier on your horse by changing your position a little bit to reflect your request.

Haunch Turns

Before doing haunch turns in the saddle, double check on the ground that you can do a haunch turn. Refer to the haunch turn section under Basic Cues to have further instruction for practicing this task. This will help your horse's understanding once you are in the saddle asking for the haunch turn and will set you up for success.

For this example we will be doing a haunch turn to the left which means the horse's front end will be moving to the left so the horse should be pivoting on the left hind foot.

Steps to completing a haunch turn in the saddle to the left:

1. In the saddle first decide on your ideal cue. Start by bringing the right leg slightly forward and add pressure; just be sure not to bring your leg too far forward because then it will make advancing and building on this skill more difficult. To increase the cue, pick up the left rein and use an open rein to turn the horse's head and shoulder slightly to the left. Use the right rein as brakes, only adding pressure with the right rein if the horse is moving forward.

2. With each step you should soften before you ask for another step. So you will be using your leg and rein on opposite sides (for the example above the right leg and left rein) and using the opposite rein as brakes (for the example above the right rein).

Knowing this skill can help when advancing skills to include performing roll backs, pirouettes, haunches in and 10-metre canter circles.

Trouble Shooting:

Problems with the haunch turn are very similar to that of the forehand turn. The most common is too much pressure in the horse's mouth. This is often expressed by the horse in one of two ways: 1) opening the mouth while raising its head trying to avoid the bit or 2) backing up. When you experience these problems, keep pressure in the mouth but use less; then add more leg as needed. Be patient and wait for the correct response, then reward by simply sitting and taking a moment to relax.

Haunch Turn

1.

1. Andrea brings her left leg forward, and opens her right rein to ask Lora for the haunch turn to the right. You can see Lora starting to move her right front leg towards the right. Lora's high head and ears really focused on Andrea suggest that Lora is still new to the haunch turn under saddle.

2. Lora starts to settle into the haunch turn and now has a much more relaxed expression and lower head set. Andrea has also softened her cues back to her ideal cue. You can see her leg is no longer quite as far forward.

2.

3. Andrea demonstrates a common error riders do when asking for the haunch turn. She is showing us how many riders will drop their rein (right hand) and try to pull the horse on the turn. Riders need to remember to lift the horse through the turn and keep their shoulders square (like in pictures 1 & 2).

3.

4.

4. After completing the turn Andrea allows Lora a chance to relax and think about the turn. You can see Lora still has one ear on Andrea waiting for the next cue. Allowing time for the horse to think is so important when training horses.

Occasionally the horse can become confused because of the rider's position. Position your body to encourage the movement you want i.e. shift your weight in the direction you want to go. This will help make the objective clearer to the horse. If you sit perfectly square in the saddle with no difference in your weight or balance, then the horse can get confused thinking, 'Isn't this how they sit when we are going straight?' Make things easier on your horse by changing your position a little bit to reflect your request.

Side Pass/Leg yielding (going sideways)

Before practicing sideways in the saddle, practice sideways on the ground by using an ideal cue similar to what your leg can do in the saddle. Follow sideways through direct pressure under 'Basic Cues' for further direction on how to do this. Once you can do 10 to 15 steps sideways with ease on the ground, you are ready to try in the saddle. You can stand your horse in front of a wall to stop him from walking forward if needed.

For this example we will be side passing to the left.

Steps to going sideways in the saddle to the left:

1. Start by adding pressure with the right leg to push the horse to the left, with each step you should soften before you ask for another step.

2. If the horse walks forward then stop the motion in front by using both reins. You can also help your horse understand this cue by gently pulling both reins back and slightly in the direction you want to go. If you want to leg yield to the left then gently pull back, while also pulling slightly to the left—being sure that the indirect rein, in this case the right rein, does not cross the mane, so pull to your belly button with the indirect rein.

3. Based on your knowledge from doing haunch turns and forehand turns (you should be able to do both haunch and forehand turns before you ask for sideways), use the appropriate cue to straighten your horse so that his body is straight when walking sideways. This means that the horse's legs will be crossing over one another.

4. Once you have mastered this at the walk, you can advance to practicing this at the trot and canter.

Knowing how to side pass/leg yield your horse can be quite helpful in jumping because you can straighten your horse to the fence while still keeping your horse's body straight and thus you can jump the fence straight. The difference between going directly sideways, and leg yielding will depend on the amount of motion you allow to go forward (i.e. use your reins mostly to direct the horse in the way you wish to go with added support from your leg if you want to maintain forward movement). For this exercise explained here, we presume your horse is straight or bending slightly

Sideways

1.

2.

3.

4.

1. Andrea begins asking Lora for sideways at the trot. She is using her right leg, right indirect rein, and her left direct rein to ask Lora to move to the left. Notice how Lora is staying bent to the right, but is travelling to the left. You can see Lora doing a nice cross over with her front legs.

2. Lora continues to stay fairly straight, but you can see her hind end starting to lag behind.

3. Andrea is using more right leg and less rein to ask Lora to catch up her hind end in order to stay straight for the sideways. You can see Lora's hind end starting to cross over.

4. Andrea has managed to get Lora moving much straighter as both her hind and front legs are reaching towards the left.

in the opposite direction of travel—this is because of using your right leg paired with an indirect right rein.

Trouble Shooting:

It is common that horses will get crooked when the rider tries to manipulate the horse. Be careful to use your cues appropriately to keep the horse straight. After practicing haunch and forehand turns in the saddle, you should be aware of the cues needed to move the front and hind end of your horse. Apply this to going sideways to keep the horse straight. Therefore if going sideways your horse tends to lag the hind end behind, use your cue to move the hind over (the same as you do for a forehand turn). It is most common for horses to lead with their front end, meaning the rider is asking too much with their hand and not enough with their leg.

Practicing just a couple of steps at a time will help you have success. Horses can get flustered if you ask for too much at one time. Horses can also get flustered if you do a lot of footwork, meaning a lot of haunch turns, forehand turns, backwards, and sideways because it takes a lot of concentration and focus, so be careful to work on other things as well. You can slowly build your horse's tolerance level by doing a few more turns, backwards or sideways steps each time you ride. To start with, only do one to two haunch and forehand turns, one to two back ups and one to two sideways each direction in an entire ride. Be sure to mix up the turns and the order that you do them so your horse doesn't fall into a routine.

Jumping

Jumping your horse is something that takes patience and time. Allowing your horse the time to build confidence over fences and trust in you will ensure that he'll trust you to jump any fence, from any distance, and most importantly, he'll *want* to jump for you. When your horse wants to jump for you, he'll make the extra effort to leave all the rails up, give the best jumps, and be forgiving of rider errors.

Horses can jump with a bascule back or a hollow back. A bascule means the horse has a rounded arch over the fence and will carry motion and forward energy that will have him naturally leave the jump at the canter. A hollow back is when the horse jumps nearly straight up, going forward just enough to clear the jump and then lands straight down. The horse's head is awkwardly high and the neck arches the wrong way. The appearance of a horse jumping hollow is similar to that of a deer jumping. It is very hard to ride smoothly.

When teaching your horse to jump, it's a good idea to start either on the lunge or by free jumping. Free jumping can allow your horse to practice finding the right take off spots and striding without rider interference.

To free jump your horse, make sure you set up a safe area with safe fencing, proper footing, and nothing that your horse can get tangled with. Set up a chute so that once your horse is given a straight approach to the first jump, he can't run out on a line of fences.

Set up tall jumps parallel to the existing arena wall, only allowing enough space in-between the two 'walls' for a jump. Be careful that the horse can't sneak between the wall and the jump and potentially injure himself. Alternately, you can set up a few jump standards in a line parallel to the existing arena wall and use a rope/caution tape/ribbon to connect each standard and create a wall. Just be sure to use something that will be visible to the horse. Caution tape is great because it will break easily if he gets caught up in it, but is also highly visible. Set up your jumps, first starting with poles.

When free jumping, send your horse through the chute a few times, making sure he's warmed up and the distances between the jumps are correct. Base the stride on ten to twelve feet plus room for take off and landing. When the jumps are 3'3" you can assume about six feet for landing and six feet for takeoff. Less landing/take off space is required for smaller jumps and if the horse trots to the first fence in the line. Remember that if you start with little jumps and build to bigger jumps, you will have to adjust the space between jumps to allow for the take off and landing distances.

You can set up one or two stride combinations to start. Once your horse is more athletic and experienced, you can set up bounces (also termed an 'in and out') where the horse jumps in and out again without any strides in-between (about nine to ten feet between jumps if the horse trots in and the jumps are around two feet).

Follow these steps:

1. Start with poles so your horse can figure out the routine and warm up, then raise the last pole in your sequence to a cross rail. Be sure to remember that the distance between poles will be different when they become jumps because you have to allow for take off and landing. Use a cross rail in order to encourage your horse to find the centre of the jump. After a couple of warm up jumps, build the middle portion of the combination. Have your horse do this once or twice or until he goes through smoothly.

2. Now you can make the jump at the beginning of your combination and make sure your horse can go through smoothly at the cross rail height before raising any jumps. Once all of your jumps of the grid are set up, you can leave the first jump a cross rail and raise the other jumps in your sequence behind it. Keeping the first jump in the sequence a cross rail will keep the grid inviting and encourage your horse to be centered into the grid. This is because the lowest point of a cross rail fence is at the centre.

3. Raise one fence at a time, allowing your horse to jump the grid when you make a change, and do not advance the grid until your horse can master the preceding level.

   You can use ramp oxers (first rail lower than the second rail) to encourage a bascule (rounded form) when jumping, versus a hollow back (deer-like) jump. You can also use jumps with objects underneath to build confidence in your horse (jumping coops, flowers, planks, brush boxes, etc.).

Be careful not to over stress your horse—keep in mind his fitness level and remember that jumping is fatiguing and puts more stress on your horse than basic flat work.

With a fit horse, free jumping should be done a maximum of once per week to allow recovery and rebuild time for the horse's muscles, joints and tendons. If your horse was pushed to the limit in a free jumping session, his next exercise session should be relaxed. Do a loose rein trot with a little canter to allow him to recover and rebuild. Not allowing recovery time can strain your horse and cause injury. Encourage your horse to carry a low head set in order to stretch his back muscles.

Typically when free jumping, you will always send the horse in the same direction during a session because the jumps will be set up for one direction. Try to warm up and cool down the horse in the opposite direction that you were jumping. Also switch the direction each free jumping session in order to try and keep the work more balanced so that he doesn't develop a weak side.

Allowing your horse to jump without a rider on his back will help him to figure out his own balance and stride without worrying about rider interference. Riders can interfere in many ways with a horse's jumping and it's important that you have an experienced and capable instructor and an experienced and capable horse when you're learning to jump.

When jumping, you should be in a two-point position. This means you will stand up, fold from the hips, keep a bend in the knee, look forward, and move your hands forward towards the horse's mouth over the fence. This position keeps you in the centre of balance when the horse jumps. It also brings your hands forward, giving more length to the rein and allowing the horse to lower his head and neck to jump properly.

Common Ways Riders Interfere with Their Horses When Jumping

Reins too short: The horse can't lower his head over the fence for proper balance. Over time this may cause your horse to start refusing jumps, using speed to get over the jumps, and/or jumping hollow (straight up). Your horse needs to be free enough to arch his neck over the jump. Watch your horse jump at freedom to see how much arch he naturally jumps with.

Two-pointing too soon: This puts a lot of weight on the front end of the horse before he's had a chance to leave the ground. Over time your horse may start to refuse jumps (especially when the heights increase) or he may speed up towards the jump in order to try and jump the fence before his rider two points too soon.

Two-pointing too late: This causes you to be left behind the motion. Usually this results in the rider pulling on the horse's mouth—that is the last thing you want to do. Pulling on your horse's mouth will offset his balance and cause his hind end to land early. The results of this are knocked rails and a horse that's nervous about jumping. The next time, your horse may speed up to try and get over the jump before you get a chance to yank on his mouth. Other possibilities are that your horse will start jumping hollow, or worst of all, refusing. If you get left behind, it's important that you immediately allow slack in the rein to avoid yanking on the horse's mouth. Even the best riders may get left behind, but the important thing is to not yank when it happens.

Coming out of the two-point too soon: If you sit down before the horse has fully landed, your weight will shift the horse's balance and cause him to drop his hind end, which could cause a rail to be knocked down. Doing this often enough may frustrate your horse and cause him to start bucking after jumps. Have someone watch your two-point, and to see if your horse's tail swishes. If it does, it means your horse is frustrated and may be because you sat down too soon.

Dramatic two-points: A dramatic two-point is a really big shift in your balance/weight by throwing your hands too far forward and leaning too far forward in the two point. Changing your position over the fence too dramatically can really interfere with the horse's balance and may cause him to start speeding at jumps to clear them before you have a chance to throw your weight. Again, if you do this often enough, your horse may start refusing jumps.

Having a knowledgeable person assess your two point and jump is critical to learning how to jump with horses. It is recommended that you seek a professional and capable coach to help you develop a safe and effective two-point.

Start your horse with some of the following exercises:

1. Start with poles on the ground and standards on either side of the pole. You want to teach your horse to go through the standards and over the poles at the centre.

2. Once you can trot and canter the poles, try setting up poles about four feet apart (for an average-sized horse) and trot through a series of poles. This will help to teach the horse the proper striding, to become more athletic, and will build your horse's confidence with new situations.

3. Next, set up a small cross rail and just work on single fences until your horse is comfortable going over jumps. Approach at the trot and try your best to stay out of the horse's way. Keep your hands still and only do a very slight two-point as it should be a really small jump.

4. Once your horse is comfortable with the little cross rail, you can add a second jump nine to eleven feet away (for horses). Trot in and encourage the bounce in-between jumps. Keep the cross rails small to make it easier for the horse to figure out where to put his feet.

5. Once your horse is comfortable you can add a third cross rail to the grid of jumps about 21 feet from the second jump. This will be one canter stride. Trot into the grid of jumps and encourage the bounce and then the canter stride. Setting the jumps up in this fashion will teach the horse the proper striding and will help him focus on technique. If your horse tends to ride with a long or short stride, you can adjust the jumps accordingly. However, if you

plan to compete, you will have to meet the stride standard, so start the jumps with striding that will boost the horse's confidence and then slowly adjust the distances over several weeks until your horse is jumping the standard distances (based on a 12 foot cantering stride).

6. Mix up jumping with flat and/or ground work so the horse doesn't anticipate a routine. Be sure to allow him to walk as a reward after every successful try through the grid for the first few jumping rides. Once your horse understands the concept of the grid, you can start to build the jumps a little higher, but it is best to change up the grid and keep your horse thinking about where to put his feet and making the strides.

7. Once your horse can stay calm and willing through variations of grids (including bounces, one stride and two strides), you'll be ready to canter into a single jump. Make sure to look for the spot where your horse will take off from so that you're ready for short or long spots. At first try to stay out of your horse's way and allow him the chance to find the perfect take off spot on his own.

8. Once your horse is comfortable with cantering to the jump, try to help your horse find the distance to the fence. This takes a skilled rider who can identify take-off spots. To help, you can count down the strides in your head where you think the jump will be (3, 2, 1 and then jump). At that point you can either squeeze your legs to ask for the long spot, hold with your hands to add an extra stride, or go with the horse if it's a good take-off spot. Once you can canter single jumps successfully, you'll be ready to approach grids at the canter. This will require positioning the jumps differently than with a trot approach. When cantering into a grid (with an average horse), the bounce will be 11 to 14 feet apart for cross rails/small verticals, 24 to 27 feet for 1 stride and 34 to 36 feet for two strides.

To help with setting up jumps, you can use the following distances (ranges given for varying heights in jumps and also varying strides for each horse):

Approached in Canter (based on 12 feet per stride, plus take off and landing space):

	Pony	Horse
Bounce	10 to 12'	12 to 14'
One Stride	21 to 24'	24 to 26'
Two strides	31 to 34'	34 to 36'

Approached in Trot (distances change for each fence in the grid because of momentum picked up by the horse/pony) between jumps 1 and 2:

	Pony	Horse
Bounce	9 to 10'	9 to 11'
One stride	16 to 18'	18 to 20'
Two Strides	30'	30 to 32'

Between jumps 2 and 3 (when you trotted to the first fence):

	Pony	Horse
One Stride	19 to 21'	20 to 23'

Between jumps 3 and 4 (when you trotted to the first fence):

	Pony	Horse
One stride	20 to 22'	22 to 24'

Refusing and Rushing Fences

Horses usually refuse and rush fences because:

- Rider error (improper balance, timing, bad line to the fence, etc.).
- Lack of confidence—the fence is scary.
- Lack of confidence—the fence or take-off spot is challenging and the horse is unsure he can do it successfully.
- The horse is fatigued/sore and physically cannot jump.

It is extremely rare for a horse to refuse just because he doesn't want to jump. If your horse does refuse fences because he simply doesn't want to jump (and you are sure it is not one of the four reasons above) then you should consider why your horse does not want to jump for you. Perhaps you need to go back to the basics and build a better relationship with your horse so that he *wants* to work for you, or you may want to consider giving your horse a different discipline that doesn't involve jumping.

There are ways to address each of the reasons for refusal, and there are ways to determine the reason why your horse behaves the way he does towards jumps. They can be addressed as follows:

1. **Rider error:** If the rider is affecting the jump you'll know, because the horse will change his behaviour based on the rider. For example, if a horse is refusing because the reins are too short, making him unable to jump, your horse will either refuse and then tug on the reins, or speed to the jump and go over with a hollow back. Once you loosen the reins, your horse will start jumping calmly and willingly. If the refusal comes because of a poor set up to the fence, then make sure he gets a fair approach. If the rider two-points too early, causing the horse to refuse, then the horse will jump after the rider starts waiting for the horse.

   Remember that how you ride a fence will affect the next fence. This means if you yank on a horse's mouth over jump X, then the next fence (jump Z) he may rush or refuse, even if you correct yourself for that fence (jump Z). If you do correct yourself over jump Z, then the following jump should be normal again. Horses who experience a lot of rider error may need more correct jumps from the rider before they trust them again, but it will happen with continued correct riding from the rider.

   If you don't have anyone to watch how you're jumping and give criticism and pointers, set up a video recorder and watch yourself. If this isn't possible, then perhaps someone can take pictures as you approach and ride over the fences. It can be very helpful to look at videos or pictures for feedback.

Remember a few key tips:

- **Give a fair approach**—a minimum of three canter strides heading straight to the fence.

- **Be centered and straight to the fence**—correct any leaning or misalignment before you get to the fence.
- **Have a spot in mind**—look for the take-off spot. If you recognize a distance for take off may be long or short, then prepare yourself to two-point at the correct moment.
- **Don't choke up on the reins**—give your horse room in the reins to lower his head and use his neck to help him jump smoothly. Sometimes short reins will actually make a horse go faster.

2. **Lack of confidence—the fence is scary:** This type of refusal is easy to recognize because the horse may try and refuse, slow down, or run out several feet before the fence. The ears will be pricked towards the jump, the horse may snort, raise his tail, and his stride may become stiffer and shorter.

When the horse stops at the fence, it's important to keep him in front of the jump. Do not let him turn or go around the jump. We want to teach our horses to face what is scary and realize that it's not that scary after all. So give him a chance to settle, even sniff the jump, then turn and leave at the trot. It's important to leave at the trot, not at the walk because the horse may think you are rewarding him for stopping at the jump if you walk (we use walking as 'relax and take a break—you did a good job'—whereas trot means 'you are in work').

Trot only far enough out to give yourself room to turn back around and approach the jump at a trot. If the fence is large and requires canter, then canter or have someone else lower the jump. Approach the jump with a loose enough rein to allow the horse to jump and to ensure you stay out of the horse's way.

Repeat this step as many times as needed until the horse jumps. If you have done more than five to seven tries then you should consider lowering the fence. Once the horse has cleared the fence, allow the horse to walk and reward with a gentle rub. Give the horse a few moments to recognize the reward, and then try the fence again.

It is important that you do not smack a horse that refuses because he is scared. Smacking a scared/anxious horse will only make him more scared and more anxious, because instead of only being afraid of the jump, he'll now be afraid of you too. An anxious state of mind is not a safe one—a nervous horse turns to fight-or-flight mode and may rear, buck or bolt.

Being patient with your horse will teach him you're a respectful leader that he can trust. When you have a horse that trusts you, he'll be more willing to jump next time. By having patience and repeating this approach as many times as required, the horse will learn the pattern and will understand that you will not rush him, but also that you'll be persistent until you get what you want. The next time the horse refuses a fence it shouldn't take as many tries to get over the jump. Soon the horse will refuse less and less until he never refuses, due to his increased confidence in your relationship and leadership.

3. **Lack of confidence—too challenging**: The horse will take you to the base of the fence and may even make an effort to go over the jump by raising a foot, reaching over with his head, or by jumping the first part of a combination. When the horse refuses, make sure you keep him facing the jump. Then assess if what you are asking is reasonable and fair based on your ability, your horse's ability, the environment (footing, weather, etc.), and your horse's current condition (is your horse ill, fatigued, sore, or dehydrated?).

If what you are asking is reasonable and fair, then proceed with the steps listed above for refusing due to lack of confidence—the fence is scary (point number 2). Approach the fence, and then if you get a refusal, wait, retreat and re-approach until your horse offers to go over the fence. If the horse has refused a part of a combination, start from the beginning of the combination. If you have tried more than seven times, consider lowering the fence(s) to build up your horse's confidence. You should also be considering your position and how you may be affecting your horse. Are you jumping before your horse (two-pointing too soon)? Are you too tight on the reins? Are you throwing yourself at the fence (doing a dramatic two-point)?

4. **Your horse is physically unable to jump what you ask**: You can recognize this because your horse may be panting or sweating profusely, indicating he's fatigued. He may be limping, feel stiff, or appear off, and also he'll remain in a calm state of mind. You need to ask yourself—is the weather too hot? Does your horse have a thick winter coat that's causing him to overheat? Is he dehydrated and in need of a drink? Is he low on energy and in need of a supplement, or time off? Is he stiff or sore (stepping short and not using the full range of motion of his limbs? Is he limping or head bobbing)? You may be able to recognize an external factor when you ask yourself these questions: Is the footing okay (too muddy, too hard or too deep)? Is the tack affecting him? Is he tossing his head and swishing his tail into and at the canter (suggesting poor saddle fit)? Is a martingale too tight? Are bandages/boots secured?

If the horse is physically unable to jump then no matter how much you ask him, he'll keep refusing, even at low heights. If by any chance he does jump, he'll likely knock the fence. If you ask yourself the above questions you can pinpoint the problem and recognize the situation. If you ask a fatigued or injured horse to jump, you run the risk of crashing through the fence, falling, or causing further injury. It is dangerous.

Dealing with the Scary Stuff

Whenever you deal with anything scary, consider the principle: 'encounter, wait and revisit.' Use this with all scary or uncomfortable things such as walking over tarps, riding past a scary corner in the arena, clippers, or a scary log on a trail. Follow this same principle for all circumstances.

Steps for dealing with scary things:

1. When you recognize a horse startling, you should back off and not bully your horse toward whatever is scary. However, make sure your horse continues to face whatever is scary. Do

Above Left: Tunnel poles keep Cody straight over a cross-rail
Above Right: A rider folds too much over the oxer

Above: Alexandra doing an effective two point letting Cody jump properly
Below: Placing poles help Cody find his take-off spots

whatever it takes to keep your horse facing the scary thing, but from a distance that the horse is comfortable with.

2.   Keep the horse facing the object because you want to teach him to confront his fears, not run from them, but you earn the horse's trust by allowing him to stay at a distance where he feels safe. When the horse reaches the point of feeling unsafe, this distance becomes termed a threshold.

3.   You allow the horse to stop at the threshold where he is unsure, and then wait for him to relax or flick an ear back. This signals the horse is asking a question and looking for further direction.

4.   At this point you can back up or do a small circle and advance forward again. You may have to do this several times, but when your horse offers to walk forward past the scary thing, you will move slowly past whatever is scary rather than taking off and bolting past.

5.   When restarting the horse towards the scary object by backing up or doing a small circle, you ensure that you are only covering ground you already have been on and thus not scary, but safe to ask a horse to go on. This means you will not have a horse trying to take off with you. Plus, the next time your horse sees something scary, he'll be much more calm and will take less 'restarts' to get past it, until eventually your horse is not scared of much of anything and is 'bombproof.'

The steps to dealing with scary tools and props:

1.   When using a spray on a horse, running clippers, or doing anything he perceives as scary, stop advancing the scary object at the first sign of discomfort, but keep the object active and in the same spot until the horse is still and quiet. This means keep spraying the bottle, running the hose, running the clippers, etc. all on the same area on the horse until the horse is still. The handler must have the confidence to keep the scary object active until the horse is still. This is because the reward is in the release. If you stop touching a horse's ear because he's flinging his head about, then you teach the horse to fling his head if he doesn't want his ear touched.

2.   Once the horse is still, retreat to an area he's comfortable with. For a head shy horse this might mean retreating back to rubbing near the withers, or when bathing this could mean retreating to spraying the grass on the farthest side away from the horse.

3.   After you have allowed a moment's rest, you can advance again until the horse shows signs of discomfort, then wait and retreat once the horse is still.

4.   Continue these steps until you are able to work with the tools, props, etc. as you wish.

Using an arm extension stick can be very beneficial when doing desensitizing. This is because if you use your extension stick to rub a horse's ear, you can have more confidence to keep rubbing until the horse is still. When the horse starts to throw his head around, it will just be the stick that gets knocked by the horse and not you. You can also put scary things like plastic bags on the end of your stick to allow more practice for desensitization without having to be within kicking/striking distance of your horse.

If you are consistent with this approach, then your horse will learn the concept and be much more trusting of you, and much more honest and willing in new situations such as jumping new fences, or arriving at new trails or show barns.

Lunging

Lunging is the act of having a horse on a long lead, about 20 to 30 feet, and then sending the horse in circles at the end of the rope with the handler in the centre of the circle. The handler follows the horse with their eyes to ensure the horse keeps going, and the handler uses a whip/stick to keep the horse engaged and to keep the horse out on the circle. The idea is to ride the horse from the ground.

Lunging is not something typically practiced by natural horsemen because round abouts usually take its place. Round abouts will teach horses responsibility, which is why it is often considered more useful than lunging. However, lunging can be useful to assess a horse, enhance conditioning, to allow a 'fresh' horse to exercise, or to help with rider exercises. When lunging you should consider that it can be very boring for a horse, so try and make it more interesting by changing location in the arena, introducing hills or obstacles to go over or around, and by changing direction and speed to help mentally stimulate the horse.

Lunging can also be a great way to exercise a horse that cannot be ridden either because of a saddle sore or other physical reason that prevents him from being saddled/ridden, or because he is slowly coming back into training and you want to lessen stress and strain.

The most important aspect of lunging is to try and remember to keep the horse mentally engaged and challenge him with new things. Ideas such as: laying down a tarp and having him lunge over it, taking the opportunity to help desensitize your horse to new things by lunging with a saddle that has ropes/bags hanging from it (be sure that items are secure and attached in a safe way), or by putting a hula hoop around your horse's neck, etc. You can change your circle size, direction, speed, location, have the horse go in between barrels or obstacles, etc. Just be creative!

Offer the new object to the horse, allow them to inspect it, and have the horse follow the object if they are still unsure.

Dealing with the Scary Stuff

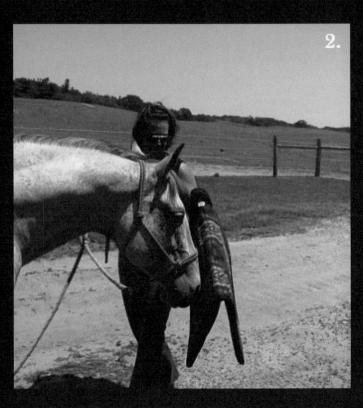

In Summary

Horses are amazing animals with a natural way of communicating with humans and each other. Horses are more than willing to follow as long as you can prove to be a strong leader who is fair, will keep them safe, and is trustworthy. Once you establish yourself as a worthy leader, your horse will offer things to you and will try to please you. You can start with basic cues that are the foundation to a language spoken through your movements that will forever evolve and develop as you play with your horse and continually learn.

Using your imagination, you can think up new puzzles for your horse to solve, or have a clear picture of what you would like your horse to perform. Having a focus is key to leading a horse because if there is no goal in mind than there is no goal at all. Your horse needs to know what you are asking and also needs to know when he has met that task.

Preserving the dignity of your horse will preserve his will, making you and your horse a strong team that will surely be a success on a trail or a force to be reckoned with in the show ring. Natural horsemanship concepts can be applied to all horses of all breeds, ages, heights, and genders participating in all disciplines at all levels with any type of rider. *There is no excuse for abuse.*

Patience and time combined with support from appropriate people will be great factors in your success. Being confident in your decision to practice naturally will play a major role in your journey with natural horsemanship and is a key to advancing with natural horsemanship. Having humility and seeking help when you face challenges beyond your comprehension is a must. Horses forgive and horses can learn new tricks.

Opening the door to natural horsemanship is opening a door with many possibilities, surprises, and a whole new positive way of working with horses in a safer, more meaningful, and more connected way. All you need to ask yourself is: Are you ready for change?

By Lindsey Forkun

Horse enthusiast since 1993, going natural since 2002

Trail Work
Never underestimate the benefits of a trail ride. Trail rides stimulate the horse in many ways and provide great conditioning for your horse too!

References

1. Rallie McAllister, MD (2006). What's the Scoop? Featuring Frederick Harper, PhD. Article 7209, Blood-Horse Publications
2. Heather SmithThomas (2008). Feeds and Supplements. Article 11404; Blood-Horse Publications
3. Kate Romanenko (2005). Dare to go Bare; Woodville, ON: Nature's Barefoot Hoofcare Guild Incorporated
4. Kate Romanenko, barefoot hoof care specialist (2005). Dare to go Bare; Woodville, ON: Nature's Barefoot Hoofcare Guild Incorporated
5. Pat Parelli (2006). Natural Horse-Man-Ship: Six Keys to a Natural Horse-Human Relationship; Western Horseman; Revised edition

CPSIA information can be obtained
at www.ICGtesting.com
Printed in the USA
BVHW051022040620
580777BV00003B/105